# Studying Science

## a guide to undergraduate success

**Also of interest**

# Catch Up Biology

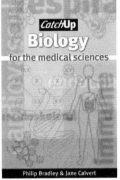

*Philip Bradley and Jane Calvert*
ISBN 9781904842323

# Catch Up Chemistry

*Mitch Fry and Elizabeth Page*
ISBN 9781904842101

# Catch Up Maths & Stats

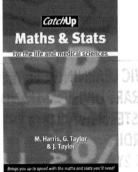

*Michael Harris, Gordon Taylor and Jacquelyn Taylor*
ISBN 9781904842118

# Studying Science

## a guide to undergraduate success

**Pauline Millican** and **John Heritage**

Undergraduate School, Faculty of Biological Sciences,
University of Leeds, Leeds, UK

Scion

© Scion Publishing Ltd, 2009

First published 2009

A CIP catalogue record for this book is available from the British Library.

ISBN 978 1904842 69 9 (*Microsoft Office 2003* version)
**ISBN 978 1904842 74 3 (*Microsoft Office 2007* version)** – this edition

**Scion Publishing Limited**
**Bloxham Mill, Barford Road, Bloxham, Oxfordshire OX15 4FF**
www.scionpublishing.com

**Important Note from the Publisher**

The information contained within this book was obtained by Scion Publishing Limited from sources believed by us to be reliable. However, while every effort has been made to ensure its accuracy, no responsibility for loss or injury whatsoever occasioned to any person acting or refraining from action as a result of information contained herein can be accepted by the authors or publishers.

Typeset by Phoenix Photosetting, Chatham, Kent, UK
Printed by Athenæum Press, Gateshead, UK

# Short Contents

# Detailed Contents

# Preface

This book has a long pedigree. For a number of years, on gaining a place at the Leeds University Medical School, students were given a short "study skills" booklet. This proved very successful and David Bullimore, its creator, very generously allowed his guide to be adapted for new microbiologists. The first of these guides was presented to new undergraduates reading Microbiology in 1995. Each year, feedback from students was actively sought and the guide evolved accordingly. With the merger of the former Department of Microbiology into a larger structure, the focus of the skills guide changed again. It then grew into a Faculty-wide skills guide with major input from colleagues, notably Linda Bonnett, as acknowledged over the page. It also morphed from a booklet to an intranet site. At that point, it was suggested that the material should be expanded to cover help and guidance for success in a life science degree, all the way from gaining a place until graduation.

The University of Leeds has a very large Faculty of Biological Sciences and consequently we see students encountering a very wide range of problems. With a few exceptions, most of these can be minimized by following faithful and familiar remedies. These experiences have contributed substantially to the advice in this book. We have also found that when helping students with problems, it has been very useful to be able to direct them to the Leeds Study Skills Guide. We feel that now is a good time to share our experience and advice with those who are about to embark on a science degree at other universities. That is probably why you are holding this book at the moment. We hope that you will find it as useful as so many of our past students at Leeds have done.

The IT material in the appendices also arose out of a tried and tested format, originally delivered in a series of "Arts Computing" modules given by Peter Millican at the University of Leeds. Over many years of teaching computing skills to non-specialists, he developed teaching materials combining general techniques with lesser-known tips and shortcuts that had proved useful to students. We are grateful for the material he provided, which has here been substantially augmented and further developed for students studying biological sciences.

*Pauline Millican and John Heritage*
Leeds, February 2009

# Acknowledgements

Many people have provided help and advice in the preparation of this book. David Bullimore is due particular thanks, for his sound introductory advice given to many cohorts of new students arriving at university over the years; without his generosity, this book could not exist. We would also especially like to thank Linda Bonnett and Peter Millican who gave generously of their ideas and time, and contributed towards several sections of the book; without their assistance, this book would have looked very different. We are grateful to many colleagues: David Adams and Celia Knight for encouraging us to get this project off the ground, Jerry Knapp, Stevie McBurney, Sue Whittle, David Pilbeam, John Grahame, John Walker, Mitch Fry, Linda Wilson and Danni Strauss, for their help during the preparation of the book. There may be others whom we may have inadvertently omitted; it is not that we are not grateful – it is just that this has been such a long project that not everyone's contribution has stuck in our minds! We also want to thank David Hames for his common-sense suggestions and Jonathan Ray for his continued support during the production process. Finally, thanks must be given to Pauline Heritage, for giving her other half the time and space to work.

# Chapter 1  Starting out

Welcome to university! This book provides a guide to the skills that you will find of value if you are to get the most from your undergraduate studies. It does not contain any magic formula that will guarantee a first class honours degree, but it does contain common-sense advice to help you to take responsibility for yourself. This advice will allow you to adapt to the challenges of university life, develop good techniques for studying, and really benefit from the opportunities on offer. A university education is about far more than acquiring a body of knowledge – it is about acquiring and practising life skills. The subject-specific, vocational, and 'transferable' skills acquired during university are all vital in equipping modern graduates for successful careers.

Some of the important skills you will need to develop include the following:

- **Personal skills:** such as organizing your work, taking responsibility for your own learning, and learning from others. You must become able to work independently and effectively and practise reviewing your personal development.
- **Managing your learning:** which means being able to reflect on how you learn and being positively self-critical in order to see how you can improve on your own performance.
- **Time management:** being organized and efficient with your time will enable you to be more successful in completing the set tasks, with time left over for relaxation.
- **Retrieval and handling of information:** finding out where to find things out.
- **Problem-solving and critical analysis:** you will find many opportunities to practise solving academic problems during your course. Critical analysis involves evaluation of other people's work, and of your own efforts, in order to decide how reliable or trustworthy various sources of information are. While practising these, you will also enhance your reasoning skills and develop your numeracy (covered in detail in *Catch Up Maths & Stats*).
- **Communication skills:** including producing written, oral and visual presentations.
- **Teamwork:** this is vital for your future career, whatever you decide to do. Often your practical work will involve collaboration with at least one person and sometimes you will work in larger groups.

Developing your ability in the skills listed above will come naturally if you become effective at the tasks and activities normally associated with completing an undergraduate course. Therefore, this guide contains hints and tips on important topics such as

- taking notes in lectures
- contributing to tutorials
- writing essays

- making the most of practical classes
- summarizing/extracting information
- using libraries effectively
- revision skills
- coping with examinations, in particular how to answer questions appropriately

## 1.1 The transition to university life

You probably have mixed feelings about the start of your undergraduate career. You might feel proud to be a part of *my* university, excited about the course you will study, looking forward to meeting new friends, and to enjoying a wide range of cultural experiences. You may also feel very daunted at the prospect of leaving home to become independent for the first time in your life; being in charge of your own finances, accommodation and catering – all of this can be scary at first. You may believe that everyone else knows so much more than you do about almost everything. But remember – it is very likely that they are experiencing exactly the same emotions as you!

More mature students and those with non-standard routes to higher education can feel just as daunted as those coming straight from school. Whatever route you have taken to get here, however, the most important thing to remember is: **DON'T PANIC.** Your worries are perfectly normal, and the best way to overcome them is to turn them to your advantage. Just think about all the interesting people you will meet and from whom you can learn much.

Whatever your background, it is probable that most of the teaching that you have received has been delivered in small groups, probably less than 30 of you, by a teacher who knew you, and whom you came to know well too. Although you may receive some small group teaching at university, for much of the time you are likely to be taught in lectures, possibly with several hundred other students. You may have never seen the lecturer before, and you may never come across that particular individual again. This may be disorienting at first, but you will find that you get used to it very quickly.

One of the greatest privileges of a university education is that you have the opportunity to learn about far more than just the subject you came to study. You will mix with and make friends with students studying diverse disciplines and you will have many opportunities to join a variety of societies and clubs. Taking an active part in such social activities is all part of discovering about the world, and you should bear in mind the old saying "*all work and no play…*".

Below is a short essay entitled "Fresher pressure" adapted from an original by Hannah Jones, a Leeds Biochemistry graduate. It says it all!

> *There can be few more stomach-churningly terrifying ordeals than coming to University. Leaving home is your final break from childhood, and nothing prepares you for it. As you begin to embrace the horrors of launderettes, supermarket shopping and using an oven, you experience pangs of fondness for your parents which you may never have imagined possible.*

*Years later, as you and your bosom buddies will pack up your posters and fight over who keeps the ironing board, once used as a tennis net, you'll look back on your early student days and laugh as you remember those crippling nerves.*

*But when you first leave your beloved homestead for the big smoke, it can be hard to think rationally about the coming months. Everyone will have offered you well-meaning words of wisdom about those early weeks, but don't believe a word of it. Let me dispel at least one myth...*

*... You'll think that you will never find any friends like the ones to whom you bid a fond farewell in the days before your departure. You decide that you'll never meet anyone who shares your love of handball and the "nonny no" madrigal, and that your new flatmates will make a joint decision that they all hate you, sneaking away behind your back for marvellous nights out while you're in the shower or engaged in a stiff upper lip telephone conversation with your mother.*

*This is pure, but understandable, paranoia on your part – as you will realize about three weeks into term time as you stagger home from a club singing "Take Me Home Country Roads" with all your other mates from the Handball Society. Even though the University community can seem the size of your entire home county, it does mean that you never have too far to go to find someone with similar interests to yourself.*

*The one true thing you're likely to be told about University is that you will meet your friends for life during these few years. Though it may take a time to find them – never fear, you will!*

## 1.2  How degrees are awarded

Traditionally, degrees in UK universities were awarded after a period of study, with the classification of degrees being dependent on a single set of examinations – finals – although some institutions did vary slightly from this pattern, with performance outside finals contributing a small amount to the final degree classification. Typically, success rested on a student's performance in the two or three weeks of these finals examinations. Any mistakes made would be reflected in the class of degree that was awarded. While this model served most people well, it could have devastating consequences for a small minority.

The time taken to complete a degree varies. Within the UK, the honours degree programmes in universities in England, Wales and Northern Ireland typically take three years, unless students opt for a fourth year to develop their professional skills in industry or elsewhere, or in studying abroad. Scottish institutions, however, have always been different because the secondary school system never included "A" levels, having a broader approach that culminated in the award of Highers. This means that students in Scotland moving to their university have a broader base on which to build their tertiary education but, it could be argued, they lack the depth of training fostered by "A" levels used in the rest of the UK (and elsewhere). An important consequence of this is that, traditionally, Scottish honours degree programmes are four years long. Another significant difference between degrees from Scottish universities and these from elsewhere is that the fourth year of study in a Scottish university is the "honours" year. While most students take this route, a few exit after three years with an "ordinary" degree. An ordinary degree from a Scottish university is thus an honourable exit – for other UK universities, people who are awarded ordinary degrees have not made sufficient progress to achieve a degree with honours. Candidates with suitable qualifications from elsewhere may be able to negotiate direct entry into Level 2 of selected degree programmes in Scottish universities.

### 1.2.1 *Modules*

In recent years, higher education has undergone a revolution, particularly in the way degree subjects have been taught and examined and "modularization" has been introduced. In modular degrees, programmes are divided into bite-sized chunks (modules) that are delivered and examined largely independently of one another. This system fits some programmes better than it does others and in science it is probably not desirable to treat all information as discrete packets. Consequently, as you progress through a particular programme of study you will find that programmes at higher levels will require that you have taken and usually passed certain "pre-requisite" modules from lower levels.

Each module is allocated a certain number of credits, which reflect the amount of work required to complete that module. Typically, at all levels, the academic year is divided into modules worth a total of 120 credits – occasionally, programmes may have more credits, particularly in those programmes that run field courses in vacations. Different universities use different weightings to modules and there is a wide variety of credit ratings.

### 1.2.2 *Semesters*

Along with modularization, most UK universities adopted "semesterization" – splitting of the academic year into halves, or "semesters". Typically, students take modules worth 60 credits in each semester, although individual programmes may allow some flexibility in the number of credits taken in each semester. The academic year may be front-loaded, with students taking 70 credits in the first semester, leaving just 50 credits to be taken in the second semester. Alternatively, the year may be back-loaded, with 50 credits being taken in the first semester and 70 credits being taken in the second semester.

### 1.2.3 *Credits*

Throughout your degree, you will be required to gain a certain number of credits by passing specific modules. Even a student who scrapes a bare pass is awarded all of the credits for that module. The actual number of marks achieved in each module is usually derived from both in-course assessment and end-of-module examinations. The relative weightings of these will vary between modules but this information will be published, so that you can monitor your progress through the degree scheme.

### 1.2.4  Degree classification

Universities differ in how they calculate the final degree classes but typically only results from study at Levels 2 and 3 contribute to the final degree classification. At Level 1, generally all that is required is for students to pass the requisite number of modules to progress. You should check for yourself exactly what your university does.

Most students graduate with honours. Those who fail a small number of modules at either Level 2 or 3 may have successfully completed sufficient modules to be awarded ordinary degrees. Where there have been significant failures and even an ordinary degree is beyond the grasp of students, they may be eligible for the award of a Diploma or a Certificate of Higher Education. Diplomas are often awarded to those who have sufficient achievement at Level 2; Certificates are for those whose achievement is confined to Level 1 work.

Honours degrees are divided into different classes: first, upper second, lower second and third class. An upper second class degree may be referred to as a 2(i) and a lower second class degree as a 2(ii). While many students aspire to first class honours, the crucial division is between upper and lower second class honours degrees. This is because to qualify for registration for a doctoral programme, an upper second class degree is the cut-off for support from most sources of funding.

Degrees that are classified as 2(ii)s are also known affectionately as "Desmond's" after Desmond Tutu, the Archbishop of Cape Town. Third class degrees may be referred to as "Richard's" (after Richard III) and in the 1980s and early 1990s were known as "Douglas's", after Douglas Hurd, the Home Secretary then Foreign Secretary at the time.

### 1.2.5  University standards

To ensure that the quality of degrees is maintained and that the standard of degrees is similar across universities, there are several checks in the system. The most important is the appointment of external examiners – senior academics with broad and deep experience of teaching and assessment. It is their job to approve degrees and to report to the university on the quality of the examination process. External examiners highlight any issues that may require attention and provide advice on new modules and programmes. Additionally, universities have internal self-review schemes and they are periodically reviewed by external assessors.

The aims of your degree programme are to provide you with a wide knowledge of your subject, to give you an appreciation of its latest research and future direction, and to prepare you for your future career.

# Chapter 2 Your degree – preparation for a career

What influenced your decision to embark on a degree course? Was it because:

- you felt that you need a degree in order to get a good job?
- you enjoy the subject and want to discover more?
- you wanted to get away from home and become independent?
- all your friends were going away to university and you didn't want to be left behind?
- you wanted to experience student life?

You may feel that all of these apply to you, but it is not really necessary to go to university to leave home and gain your independence, or to find a job where you work and have fun with people of a similar age. Taking a degree course involves a lot of time, hard work and, inevitably at times, a great deal of anxiety. In addition, there will be the strong possibility that by the end of it you will be in considerable debt.

Now ask yourself: what do I want to *get out* of being at university? Most students would answer:

- I want to get the best degree I can to help me get the best job that suits me, as soon as possible after I leave university
- I want to study a subject I enjoy

So the reasons that you embark on a university degree course in the first place become clearer; you want to spend your time doing something in which you are interested to help you get **the best degree result you can in order to help you have an enjoyable and rewarding career.**

How can you go about this?

The following sections in this book contain lots of information about how to work effectively and successfully at university and, if you follow the advice, you will put yourself in a very good position to do well. Doing well may not mean doing *as well* as you could, however! It would be a great shame if, having spent years of your life enjoying the privilege of being in higher education, at the end you achieve a less than satisfactory result. This section is devoted to **strategies to help you achieve to the VERY BEST of your abilities** while at university.

## 2.1 Skills for success

At university, you will have a lot more freedom to plan and structure your own work than at school or college, but you must not be tempted to socialize at the expense of your subject work. If you do, you will quickly find that you will start to fail. It is important early on that you try to get the balance right between work and socializing, to allow you quickly to establish a solid foundation on which to build your academic career. Adjusting to this self-discipline can be hard, as can be trying to understand exactly what is expected. If you find that this is the case, then do not be afraid to ask your tutors or fellow students for help and advice.

Also, bear in mind that, although at school or college you may have been able to improve the first mark you obtained in an exam or assessment by retaking it, at university this is not normally possible and your first attempt at an assessment is the one that counts. If you are allowed to re-sit a failed exam, the mark you can obtain may be capped at just the pass mark. This means that your first attempt at the exam really should be your best.

At Level 1 (your first year), the foundations are laid for your course; you will gain an overview of your subject at an elementary level and begin to develop the skills necessary to progress. These will be both subject-specific (e.g. experimental design, laboratory techniques, data presentation, etc.) and also generic (e.g. IT, time management, communication, problem-solving). By the end of this year you will be expected to know the core aspects of your subject and its principal conventions and terminology. The skills you have acquired, such as writing essays, carrying out practical exercises and producing reports, should enable you to demonstrate your knowledge and expertise in your subject.

Level 2, or second year, is where you develop your learning capabilities and explore your subject. Your knowledge and understanding will become both broader and more detailed and you will develop more independence. The subject-specific skills that you acquire are required to carry out more demanding and complex tasks as you progress.

Level 3, or third year (even if you have a study year abroad or in industry), is the time for you to consolidate your knowledge and expertise in the subject. You will be expected to explore trends in current research and be aware of possible future developments. Generally, this is the year in which you will, independently, carry out an individual research project; a challenging task but one that will help you become proficient at many of the skills you practised in the previous two years. This will give you a better view of what it is like to be a research scientist.

### 2.1.1 *Planning your study and leisure time*

OK, there's a lot going on at university and it's a shame to miss all the other activities that are part of it. How do you study effectively and still have time to do other stuff?

#### Good planning is the key to success

Ask yourself "How do I plan my study time?" Is it weekly, monthly, termly or even yearly? All answers could be correct depending on what you are doing. Successful students plan by a combination of all of these, using the week as the basic unit for essays, reports, worksheets etc., but bearing in mind events and deadlines on a longer timescale, such as examinations and projects. Ideally, you should:

- keep a diary and/or compile a weekly chart to use as a timetable, such as the one shown below (Figure 1.1). Why not produce your own template using a word processor? You will find an explanation of how you can produce tables easily using *Microsoft Word* in *Appendix A, Section 3.7*.

- enter all your lectures, practical classes and tutorials into your diary and/or onto the grid to help you to plan when you are going to fit in the time for your private study.

- try to arrange your study at times when you are most receptive to learning. Are you a lark or an owl? Some people work best early in the day (the larks), whereas others are most receptive at night (the owls).

- do **not** try to burn the candle at both ends on a regular basis; it becomes counter-productive ***very quickly***.

- if you think you need active reminders of forthcoming deadlines or meetings you may find that facilities such as the "Taskmaster" function in *Microsoft Outlook* are useful, because it can be set to alert you at specific dates and times.

| | Weekly Plan – Week Beginning: __/__/__ | | | | | | |
|---|---|---|---|---|---|---|---|
| | Mon | Tue | Wed | Thu | Fri | Sat | Sun |
| 06.00–08.00 | | | | | | | |
| 08.00–09.00 | | | | | | | |
| 09.00–10.00 | | | | | | | |
| 10.00–11.00 | | | | | | | |
| 11.00–12.00 | | | | | | | |
| 12.00–13.00 | | | | | | | |
| 13.00–14.00 | | | | | | | |
| 14.00–15.00 | | | | | | | |
| 15.00–16.00 | | | | | | | |
| 16.00–17.00 | | | | | | | |
| 17.00–18.00 | | | | | | | |
| 18.00–19.00 | | | | | | | |
| 19.00–20.00 | | | | | | | |
| 20.00–21.00 | | | | | | | |
| 21.00–22.00 | | | | | | | |
| 22.00–23.00 | | | | | | | |
| 23.00–24.00 | | | | | | | |
| 24.00–01.00 | | | | | | | |

**Figure 1.1 Timetable for study and leisure**

### 2.1.2 How much work should I do?

The amount of work that you do from week to week will vary, sometimes quite considerably. On average, however, you should find that your total fixed work commitments for the week should be about 40–45 hours. If you find that you *regularly* need to work for more than 50 hours a week, then you should discuss your work patterns with somebody: friends or classmates, your personal tutor, or another member of staff. You may need advice on learning techniques, or you may have unrealistic ideas about what is actually expected. To help you to get your balance of work correct, you might like to include planned leisure activities, such as sport, society events, or just meeting up with friends, on the timetable as well. These will give you times in the week to which you can look forward.

Use planning timetables sensibly and remember that they should only be used for guidance *not* as rigid timetables that dominate your life. Being flexible is necessary when you have several assignments due close together and you will have to devote considerably more time to your studies than at other times. Remember, too, that this may happen at the end of term when there is considerable pressure to socialize. To make the best use of your time, you should review the *actual* time that you spend doing things, and compare this with your *planned* timetable. Essays, for example, frequently take far longer to prepare and write than you might anticipate. Reviewing your progress will help you to get the balance right when planning future timetables. Besides planning your weekly schedule, you might like to consider using a chart for the whole year. This will help you to avoid being caught out by deadlines for assessments and examinations that otherwise have a nasty habit of creeping up on you. You should plan for your leisure, too: socializing is very important and it can be a great incentive to get work out of the way and then to let your hair down and celebrate.

### 2.1.3 Effective private study is an essential part of your course because ...

- it helps you to reinforce the information and to understand the concepts presented to you in lectures and practical classes and to prepare for assessed in-course tests
- regular private study will reduce the pressure on you when it comes to the exams, as you will have done much of the groundwork
- it will increase your understanding and, hopefully, your enjoyment of your subject
- the ability to structure your own time effectively is an invaluable life skill

More detailed advice is given later on how to make the most of the teaching sessions at university but there are two "golden rules" to remember for effective private study.

### 2.1.4 Golden rule 1 – plan your time

Set aside some time for study and then get on with it. Remember, *"procrastination is the thief of time"*. If your room is not conducive to study because it is noisy or your friends keep calling round for coffee then go to the library.

### 2.1.5  *Golden rule 2 – use the time effectively*

Here are a few tips to help you to achieve this in lectures, tutorials, and practicals.

## Lectures

- After each lecture, you should read through the notes/handout. Make a summary. If there's something you don't understand, look it up in one of the recommended textbooks. If you still don't understand, ask for help. Stupid questions are those that don't get asked.
- Repeat the process at the end of a lecture block. Can you summarize the key points of this set of lectures? Summarizing what you know makes an excellent resource for revision.
- Make use of resources on the internet – but make sure you can trust the sources of the information that you use.

## Tutorials

- Be prepared for tutorials – complete any preparation work beforehand and hand in, **on time**, any homework for the next session.

## Practicals

- Try to read through the relevant notes before you go to the lab session. You may not understand everything at this point but it will give you some idea of what the practical is about and this will increase your understanding and the amount of benefit you get from it. You will also **get it done more quickly**.
- Write up practical reports and **hand them in on time**. A poor/incomplete record of practical work is the best way to fail the module.

### 2.1.6  *And finally… the responsibility for learning rests on you*

Lecturers and demonstrators are anxious to help you and want you to enjoy the course, but can do little if you are not prepared to make the effort. Interest often comes through understanding.

## 2.2  Help!

Things do go wrong. When you start your undergraduate course, you are embarking upon a new life. Adjusting to a new subject and a new way of studying is not easy. It can be daunting and many students find it difficult at the outset. Don't be discouraged – ask for help. Remember that…

> *…asking for help is not a sign of weakness, it is good common sense.*

Most universities recognize that it is reassuring to students to have a member of staff whom they get to know well. Most universities run a **personal tutor system** where the tutor will meet students regularly, particularly during the early part of your course. This enables students to get to know their personal tutor quickly and so should be able to turn to him/her if general difficulties arise. Alternatively, you may feel happier talking to another member of staff. It is usually easy to spot the people who will be sympathetic to this approach.

### 2.2.1 *Where else can you ask for help?*

If you are having difficulties with your studies a fellow student may be an appropriate source of support, but it may be better to talk to a member of the teaching staff. You can always take your academic problems to the person running the module. On a personal level, it may be that a chat with a friend will sort things out. A quick phone call home can work wonders, too.

In every academic year, many students suffer from 'flu-like illnesses, as people from all over the world arrive at university in the autumn, bringing with them their "local" viruses. This will almost inevitably lead to absences from some classes. Do not forget to copy up the notes of lectures that you have missed from a friend who is willing to lend you a *good* set of notes. Your tutors will be sympathetic to *genuine cases* and will expect you to report absences as soon as possible after your return, or by phoning when you are still away. This is particularly important if you are likely to be off for more than a couple of days.

Do remember to register with a local medical practice when you arrive at university. Although you may wish to register with a local General Practitioner (GP), most universities have a student medical practice that offers the full range of general practice services, and provides the same high degree of confidentiality as your GP at home. In addition, the doctors in university practices have a very wide experience of dealing with "student" problems.

#### Dear John... the agony aunt page

> *Dear John,*
>
> *I have got a "friend" who seems to be losing interest in the course. He is really bright but all he does is slob around the flat watching daytime telly. He exists on takeaways and cans of beer. I know that he is going to fail the year if he carries on like this. What can I tell him he should do?*
>
> *Worried of Woodhouse*

Uncle John's advice:

When your "friend" starts getting turned off it is *REALLY IMPORTANT* that he should see his personal tutor or *someone* on the academic staff *as soon as possible*. It may be that he just needs to chat about his situation and about life in general. Find a person who can help your "friend" to make the best decision for **him** about **his future**.

If your "friend" stops attending and gives up on course work then some pretty unpleasant things will start to happen. Your "friend" will get letters sent to him, inviting him for a chat (i.e. he will have to explain his behaviour). If your "friend" ignores these approaches, he will get letters from the university authorities. If, foolishly, your "friend" ignores these, or fails to convince the powers that be that he really has tried hard, then he will be kicked out. Imagine how his parents will feel about the support and money they have invested!

What your "friend" must do is talk to someone before the problem becomes a tragedy. Remember, in the words of H. G. Wells, "... *failure is not failure nor waste wasted if it sweeps away illusion and lights the road to a plan*".

# 2.3  Personal Development Portfolios

Many university departments encourage their students to maintain a Personal Development Portfolio (PDP). As its name suggests, the aim of a PDP is to encourage students to get into the habit of thinking about and keeping a record of their personal development so that they become more aware of their own strengths and weaknesses. This means reflecting on performance in all aspects of both academic progression and also personal skills (such as the ability to communicate well, to present information clearly and in an appropriate form, and to work well in a team), recognizing strengths so that they can be built on, and identifying weak areas so that efforts can be made to improve in them.

## 2.3.1  *Why should you keep a PDP?*

If you take a reflective attitude to your personal development you will be taking responsibility for your learning, and you are more likely to take full advantage of the opportunities available at university for developing your knowledge and skills. This will achieve one of the aims of higher education – to become an independent learner. You will also be much more likely to reach your potential, because only *you* can truly identify the weaknesses that need to be addressed, and only *you* are truly able to organize your time to set about improving those areas. Being in control of your own learning will make you more aware of your abilities, more self-reliant, and also more capable; attributes that most employers will be looking for in prospective graduate employees. In addition, when it comes to writing your *curriculum vitae*, or CV for short, a PDP will be invaluable for reminding you of your achievements and skills.

To get a good idea of the types of skills and attributes that are valued by employers, you only have to look through adverts for jobs. A report published in 2008 entitled '*Graduate Employability: What do employers think and want?*' by Will Archer and Jess Davison includes a list of attributes that employers most want in new graduates. An adapted version of the top ten is reproduced below:

- communication skills (written and oral)
- team-working skills (and cooperation skills)
- integrity (honesty, dependability and reliability)
- intellectual ability
- confidence (enthusiasm and energy)

- character/personality (self-motivation, commitment, a willingness to learn and a 'can-do' attitude)
- planning and organizational skills (including time management, punctuality, and the ability to meet deadlines)
- literacy (having good writing skills and being able to assimilate written information with ease)
- numeracy (being good with numbers)
- analysis and decision-making skills

When developing your PDP, you should consider how you match up to these criteria. If your university has not organized a PDP scheme for the students, don't let that stop you having a go on your own. The advice below will help you take the initiative for your personal development.

### 2.3.2  How to keep a PDP

Start thinking strategically:

- identify what you want to achieve and find out what you have to do to achieve it
- evaluate your progress regularly (after a set time: a term, a semester, a year) to see whether you are on course to achieve what you want
- be honest with yourself and do not compromise
- if you are not satisfied with your progress in a particular area, look for resources to help and be prepared to spend extra time on developing your skills in that area
- don't procrastinate – just do it!

This process requires discipline and you will need to keep a log of your progress in such areas as:

- attendance at lectures, tutorials and practicals (is it sufficient?)
- preparation for tutorials and practicals (how much do you do and is it sufficient?)
- participation in tutorials and practicals (how much do you do and is it sufficient?)
- performance in tutorials and practicals (in-course marks for essays, worksheets and practical reports – are they satisfactory?)
- academic performance: exam results (are they satisfactory?)

You could also focus on specific aspects of these areas for development, such as those required to conduct practicals successfully, as listed in the grid below (Figure 2.1). If you feel that you are not progressing satisfactorily, you will need to decide what you need to do to help yourself improve. Tabulating the log of your development, in a form similar to the grid below, will make it easy to identify areas on which you need to concentrate.

| Area for development | | 1 = very poor, 5 = very good | | | | |
| --- | --- | --- | --- | --- | --- | --- |
| | | **1** | **2** | **3** | **4** | **5** |
| Lectures | preparation | | | | | |
| | attendance | | | | | |
| | follow-up work | | | | | |
| Tutorials | preparation | | | | | |
| | attendance | | | | | |
| | participation | | | | | |
| | tutorial marks (essays, worksheets) | | | | | |
| Practicals | preparation | | | | | |
| | attendance | | | | | |
| | understanding of practical techniques | | | | | |
| | working with a partner or within a team | | | | | |
| | organizational skills | | | | | |
| | time management | | | | | |
| | quality of practical results | | | | | |
| | analysis of results | | | | | |
| | practical marks | | | | | |
| Exam results | | | | | | |

**Figure 2.1  Suggestion for a development log**

In addition, you should keep a record of the extracurricular activities in which you have taken part. Being the chair, secretary or treasurer of a university club or society shows that you are a reliable and responsible person, in addition to having a life 'outside' your chosen subject. This is especially important if you go into a job unrelated to your subject of study. You should ALWAYS keep a record of all your examination results. Now let's explore how to get the most from your degree programme.

# Chapter 3 How to learn in a university setting

## 3.1 The learning process: "deep" and "surface" learning

Which method of learning do **you** use?

| Method A | Method B |
|---|---|
| "I get down most of the bullet points from the *PowerPoint* presentations and I try to remember those" | "I try to find the main principles underlying new knowledge and try to fit them into what else I know" |
| "I find cramming for exams suits me. I only need to remember the things that I've learned the day before the exam. Otherwise studying just gets in the way of my social life" | "I try to find practical examples for new material. This can be difficult, but these flashes of understanding come when it all drops into place. Then it just becomes part of what you **know**" |
| "I collect loads of facts, and keep on writing them down. Then, in the exams, I fit the facts to the questions and hope for the best" | |

*"... and if you could use only one, which would you choose?"*

**Surface learning** is an approach to learning in which the detail of information in a text or lecture is memorized and is typified by Method A.

**Deep learning** is characterized by placing the focus on the overall structure of information, and the way that it fits into and extends an existing framework of knowledge and understanding. It looks at a big picture, and fits more knowledge to it to make an even bigger picture, as described in Method B.

Either approach is likely to lead to reasonable results until you start as an undergraduate. *From now on, however, surface learning is less and less likely to lead to success.* Sometimes, a shallow approach to learning may be OK, but the volume and complexity of the new material that you will come across means that, to be successful, you will need to take an in-depth approach to your studies.

To engage in deep learning involves some effort, particularly if you are not familiar with the methods employed. **Persevere with it!** The more you practise deep learning, the easier it becomes.

Independent research has shown that *without exception* students whose work was of a sufficient standard to earn a first or upper-second class honours degree used a deep approach to learning. Students who are awarded third class honours all use surface learning. What more can we say?

# 3.2 Individual study – how do students learn?

Individual study will certainly form a major part of your learning at university. Because of this, you will need to find the answers to questions such as "where?", "when?" and "for how long?" do you need to study on your own. This section is devoted to individual study, how to go about it and the potential problems that you may encounter.

### 3.2.1 *Where to study?*

You need to find places to work in which you feel comfortable and, importantly, where you are able to concentrate. You must also be able to have your books and other study materials around you such as in a study-bedroom, a flat, or in one of the libraries. If you use your own room, set it up to suit your needs, with adequate light and heating, and your books, files, etc. close to hand. Many people find that it helps to have one area devoted to study. It is also a good idea to separate the area in which you study from the area in which you sleep. You need quality rest, particularly when working very hard, for example, in the run-up to examinations. Enjoy the time that you spend in social areas such as coffee bars, bars, and the student common rooms, but *never fool yourself that these are places for serious study*.

### 3.2.2 *When to study?*

The question of when to work is best defined by your experience of your own working pattern. Having studied hard for university entrance, you will probably know at what times you work best. Make these times your prime times, and make sure that you use at least some of your prime time on most days for a concentrated period of study without any intrusion of other activities.

Whatever time of the day or night that you work, you must ensure that you get enough sleep. If you regularly work from six to eight in the morning that is fine, but it is a terrible idea if you regularly stay up until past midnight as well.

### 3.2.3 *For how long should you study?*

Learning is an active process and few people can really concentrate for more than an hour at a time without a break. *Plan* short five- or ten-minute breaks in your study, every so often, where you have a cup of coffee or tea, talk to your pet piranha, or go out for a breath of fresh air. These breaks will renew your concentration, refresh you, and make you more receptive to new material.

Plan how long you intend to spend at a particular study session, and try roughly to stick to it. You may find it useful to use the timetable approach outlined earlier. This is particularly useful in the first few weeks of the course, when you need to establish your new work pattern. Fill in your fixed commitments, and then hatch in the additional hours that you intend to study.

### Be realistic

If the planning approach is going to succeed, then you must be honest about how long you really need to spend studying in order to make sure that you are not being left behind. But also remember that you should not spend every waking hour studying to the exclusion of everything else; a university education should be about much more than obtaining a degree in your chosen subject.

## 3.2.4  *Should you study by topic or by time?*

You should try to study by topic, rather than for a certain time. Don't aim to study for *"two hours"*, but aim *"to understand and be able to draw out the Krebs cycle"*. This topic study approach should be an active approach with realistic goals. Write down what you want to start with, list the main points that you want to learn, then sketch in the more detailed bits. You can divide the knowledge into levels: "must know", "should know" and "nice to know". For the Krebs cycle it might look something like the table below.

**Table 3.1 "Must know", "should know" and "nice to know" information**

| "Must know" | "Should know" | "Nice to know" |
|---|---|---|
| The framework of knowledge to understand the topic and proceed further. "Must know" may include information such as "… the Krebs cycle is a major energy-yielding pathway. When the Krebs cycle doesn't work, you end up getting cramps". This is "must know" for all serious students of biological sciences, but probably not all that you will need to know about this topic. | Knowledge that adds breadth to your learning, and will help to bring topics together. For example, "should know" information may be "… the Krebs cycle is also known as the citric acid cycle, or the tricarboxylic acid or TCA cycle". This will help you look up alternatives in book indices where only one name may be used. If you are a biochemist, "must know" information will also include "…the enzymes involved and the metabolic components of the Krebs cycle: citrate, *iso*-citrate, $\alpha$-ketoglutarate, succinyl CoA, etc". For the rest of us mere mortals, this is probably just "should know" or even "nice to know" information. | Knowledge that may be an anecdote or a piece of history. Who *was* Hans Krebs anyway? You can easily survive without "nice to know" knowledge, but it comes in very handy for trivia quizzes. |

When you are close to the end of an individual study session, take a few minutes to review what you have covered. Try to tie it in with what you already know, and with other things that you have been studying recently. This will help you to build up an overall picture of your subject, and will greatly improve your understanding. *The more that you practise this, the easier it gets.*

# 3.3 Effective reading

You will undoubtedly need to spend a large amount of time 'reading for your degree'. The sheer bulk of reading matter to which you might be directed during your courses can be overwhelming. This will come in a variety of guises, including Recommended Reading, Key References, Reading Lists, Directed Reading Lists, or General References. *You will not have time to read all of these,* nor will you be expected so to do. Much of the material that has been suggested will be of great value to you if *you* wish to pursue a particular area in depth. By employing suitable strategies, however, you will become effective in selecting the most appropriate reading material, and decide upon the appropriate amount of detail, breadth, and depth you need. If you are unsure about what is expected of you, then always make sure that you ask what is required.

To read *effectively*, you have to be clear about your purpose. Ask yourself ..."***Why am I reading this?***" To practise, ask yourself now why you are reading this book. Are you just skimming through the text to get a "feel" for the topic, or are you reading it carefully to gain detailed information that you intend to use? Depending upon your answer to this question, your approach will be quite different. To help with serious reading, you may wish to consider the approach that is summarized by the "**SQR⁴**" approach:

| | | |
|---|---|---|
| **Scan** | – | read through for an overview |
| **Question** | – | decide what you want from your reading |
| **Read** | – | an *active* process, searching out key material |
| **Recall** | – | periodically consider what you have covered |
| **Review** | – | at the end, pull all the information together |
| **Relate** | – | tie in what you have read with other topics |

For deep learning, relating what you have read to what you already know is the most important of effective reading disciplines.

Some things are implicit in this approach.

- You should read a definite topic and not just "the next chapter" or "for half an hour" (most textbooks are not designed to be read slavishly from cover to cover).
- Try to familiarize yourself with the overall structure and content of an unfamiliar book, so that you get an overview of the subject.
- You should try to fit new material into a framework of your previous knowledge. This is how new material is most easily learned.

Academic reading is an active rather than a passive process. It is *hard work*. So, you should remember that you will read best somewhere that you can concentrate and work in comfort. Note-taking is a skill that will not only help you in lectures (see *Section 4.1*) but also in your private study. If you learn best by underlining or **highlighting** key sections of text as you read them, do not forget the **Recall, Review** and **Relate** sections of the **SQR**[4]. Remember that you must **NEVER** mark library books in this manner; only mark your own private copies of books. If you got a great deal from a book that you have borrowed, consider buying a copy for future reference.

---

### Checklist for effective reading

- Ask yourself (question) what you want to get out of your reading.
- Scan through the chapter(s) to see what the sub-headings are about.
- If the chapter has a summary, read through this more carefully, identifying the main points of the arguments that have been covered.
- Read through the introductory paragraphs carefully; these should set the scene for what is to follow.
- Select the appropriate sections and sub-sections of relevance and actively read these. Identify the main ideas in each section. These are often encapsulated in the first line of a paragraph or section, although sometimes they may be found in the last sentence.
- Study the examples that are given. Make sure that you understand how they relate to the idea of that section of text.
- Summarize periodically the main ideas and examples that you have read in your own words so that you can understand the topic. Making brief notes will help with this. Do not attempt to copy out the textbook! Simple pictures and diagrams can help to give a different slant on a topic and will help you to recall the material. Check that you have not missed anything out and that you really understand the material.
- When you have finished reading the whole topic, review what you have read. The easiest way to do this is to scan through your notes.
- Relate what you have just read to other areas of knowledge.

---

## 3.4 When the good times go bad

All this advice on how to learn sounds easy – a breeze, in fact. But there will be bad times when you don't feel like working. Nothing seems to go in, and suddenly you can't see the point of it all. Everything becomes too much bother. Being honest, these times will happen to everybody at some point. The trick is not to let the bad times last for too long. There are no magic solutions to overcoming the bad times, but here are some suggestions.

If you have difficulty in starting your work, then you should choose something constructive but straightforward. For example, you could just note down the main points of a lecture or tutorial. If you find one of the recommended textbooks hard to understand, then try looking at other books, they may have clearer explanations, or they may have better illustrations.

If you are bored with what you are studying, try dividing the topic that bores you into manageable packages, and spend time, little and often, on these smaller sections. Alternatively, you could ask a friend to teach you the topic "in the style of your favourite lecturer". Explaining topics to one another in a fun manner is an excellent way for you both to learn. Finally, you could try mild shock therapy by attempting questions off old examination papers under examination conditions. However, bear in mind that courses change with time, so you may not have the background to answer all or any of the questions on older exam papers. If you have any such problems, consult the person who runs the module about the nature of the course in the past.

None of this may work. Remember that you came to university to train as a good scientist. If things seem to be getting on top of you, discuss your problems with somebody. Members of staff are there to help you. Don't forget your friends. They will be happy to help you out, too.

# Chapter 4 Making the most of teaching

## 4.1 Learning from lectures

The one-hour lecture still dominates the teaching of many courses; especially those taught to large numbers of students. If you think a lecture is the process whereby a lecturer's notes are transferred to a student notebook without the need for mental effort on anybody's part, think again. If you approach lectures in the proper manner, you will find that you will learn a great deal from them. The benefits that you can derive from lectures include:

- providing an overview or summary of an area of interest
- highlighting and discussing difficult areas
- covering and linking subject matter that is not well covered in standard textbooks
- introducing relevant research topics, which may include recent discoveries and other advances in your subject

### 4.1.1 *How do you get the most out of lectures?*

Lectures may be given in stuffy lecture theatres, possibly in semi-darkness. This, together with the time that they occupy, can lead to them making you feel very drowsy. Large lecture classes in particular limit the opportunities for discussion, making the flow of information seem to be only one-way, from lecturer to student. However, these will not be major drawbacks if you follow the advice below and learn how to *listen*. Listening in lectures should be an active process.

### 4.1.2 *Before the lecture*

To prepare for each lecture, you should:

- read about the general area of the lecture topic *beforehand*
- spend a few minutes before the lecture trying to recall what you already know about the subject – this will help greatly with a deep learning approach to your studies
- TURN YOUR MOBILE PHONE OFF BEFORE YOU ENTER A LECTURE THEATRE
- try not to arrive late. You will almost certainly miss a very important part of the lecture – its outline. Lecturers often spend the first few minutes of a lecture introducing the subject, and placing it in the context of other lectures. In any case, being late, unless for a good reason, is impolite
- sit near to the front of the lecture theatre if possible – you should be able to see and hear more easily

- do not chat, even in a whisper, during lectures. It is very rude, and it is highly distracting for others. Some lecturers may ask you to leave if you continue to talk during their lectures. More embarrassingly, they may want to join in your conversation...
- if you can, sit with a group of students with whom you feel at ease. If your lecturer breaks up the lecture into small group discussions, then this will be much more productive, and fun, if you get along with your neighbours

### 4.1.3 Active listening

Many lecturers use a standard format for their lectures; they will have a beginning (the outline of the lecture), a middle (the body of the lecture) and an end (a summary of the points that have been covered). Recognizing this form will enable you to organize your thoughts and structure your lecture notes.

A good lecture always starts with a **preamble**, such as ... *"Hello, my name is Dr Frank N Stein"*, and this preamble is followed in a good lecture by the **orientation**. This is where the lecturer tells you what will be covered in the lecture, and, possibly, how this material relates to other subjects given in the lecture course. Your notes can then reflect this structure as below:

Lecture on SUBJECT

    Orientation

    This lecture will consider the following key points:

        Topic A, Topic B, Topic C

        Topic A ...

            Description ...

                Extension 1 to Topic A

                First example (+ aside)

                Second example (+ aside)

        Topic B ...

            Description ...

And so on ...until ...

        The summary

Taking notes in a lecture is a very personal matter, but the following basic guidelines might help you structure the material more clearly.

**Key points** are the major topics around which the lecture is structured (Topics A, B and C). You should note key points carefully, along with their **extensions**. These are the secondary areas covered in the lecture.

**Examples** provide useful illustrations related to particular points in a lecture, and **asides** are less important points. These provide light relief in a lecture, and may be humorous in nature.

**Summaries** are used to bring together different sections of the lecture. These may often begin with a phrase like... *"what this goes to show is..."*, or something like it.

Most lecturers provide opportunities for **questions** either during the lecture, or on an individual basis at the end. Don't be afraid to ask about things that you do not understand. Lecturers are there to help you to learn. Many students do not feel confident enough to ask a question in front of others during the lecture so, if you feel this way, you are not alone! However, if you are confused by part(s) of the lecture or want to know more, do go and meet the lecturer at the end and ask your questions then. Lecturers are usually very enthusiastic about their subject and welcome such student queries.

If you find that you have particular difficulties understanding an individual lecturer, because of the way the material is presented, it is a good idea to discuss these problems, if not with the lecturer concerned then with your personal tutor. Good lecturers will want to act on constructive criticism where there are positive suggestions about how to clarify the lecture material or improve the lecturing style. Do remember, however, that lecturers are human too and don't like negative criticism any more than you do, which is why constructive comments are far more likely to bring about the changes that you want.

## Tips that can help you with active listening

**Be selective:** you will not be able to take down everything in a lecture, unless you are very proficient at shorthand. If you are not selective in your note-taking, then you will miss important points, and may well end up misunderstanding the material being taught.

**Take legible notes:** it is more than likely that you will not have time to make "fair" copies of all of your notes, however much you promise yourself that you will. So, try to make legible notes from the outset. Don't forget to file any handouts with the relevant lecture notes after the lecture.

**Reinforce your note taking:** educational research has shown that when you leave a lecture theatre you will remember less than half of the content of the lecture. One week later, you will remember only half of this half. A few minutes spent in the evening of the lecture going over your notes can help to prevent the secondary loss, and this will save you much trouble later. Get into the habit of reading through your notes. To reinforce your reading, write an outline of the lecture, sketching out the main points, sub-headings and principal examples from the lecture. After you have done this, you should review your notes again, and amend your revision notes. List the points that you do not understand. If you find that textbooks do not help to clarify the problem, then ask your friends, or your personal tutor or the person who gave the lecture.

**Link the material in each lecture:** it is rare that lectures stand entirely alone. More often they occur within a module or course with common themes. It will greatly assist your deep learning if you search for and describe the links between various individual lectures, and then go on to develop links across the whole of a module or course.

## *Tips for making the most of your notes*

**Highlight essential points** as you take notes, for example by <u>underlining</u> words or using CAPITALS or \*\*asterisks\*\*. If you carry a range of coloured pens, you may also wish to change the colour of your text in your notes. When you re-read your notes you can use coloured highlight pens, but don't overdo it since you can very easily overwhelm your text with fluorescent colours.

**Compare notes** with your friends. Everybody will bring a slightly different perspective to a lecture, and so it is likely that you will gain insights into the material that may have been important to your friends but that you considered of lesser importance. By sharing notes, you will expand your experience of the lecture material. You will also reinforce your learning through discussion with others, and this will be of great benefit when you want to revise.

If you make use of the advice above, you should enjoy your lectures, and you will be able to make the most of them.

---

**Checklist for getting the most out of your lectures**

- Arrive promptly or you might miss important introductory points.
- Do not try to write down everything the lecturer says.
- Listen to what the lecturer is saying and try to follow the thread.
- Make short notes to supplement the information in your handouts, when available.
- Note down any references to resources so you can look them up later.
- Do not chat your to neighbour – you will miss information and disturb others, including the person giving the lecture.
- As soon as possible after the lecture, look over your notes to remind yourself of the contents and look up any extra information you feel you need.
- Before the next lecture, make sure you have understood the information in the previous one. If you don't, you will find it more difficult to grasp new information.

---

# 4.2 Learning from tutorials

Tutorials offer a very special opportunity for learning, since they involve small groups of students working together. In this section, tutorials refer to groups of up to about ten students talking through a topic with a tutor. Typically, tutorial sessions last for about an hour.

Providing that the participants prepare properly for a tutorial, they can be amongst the most stimulating of learning sessions. At their best, tutorials promote discussion, clarify difficult topics and permit study of a subject at a greater depth than is possible in a lecture. They give you the opportunity to express *your* views and give your knowledge an airing. You can also practise your listening skills when others are making their contribution. Furthermore, they provide social occasions when you can get to know fellow students and your tutor better.

Successful tutorials require the **three Ps – Planning, Preparation** and **Participation.** You, the student, must take an equal share with your tutor in being responsible for the three Ps.

**Planning** involves finding out what is to be discussed well in advance of the tutorial session. You should discuss this both with your tutor and with fellow students. Tutorials are generally flexible and, with advanced planning, they can be adapted to reflect your needs and interests. Without planning, preparation becomes impossible.

**Preparation** for a given tutorial will vary depending on the work to be covered in that tutorial. It may require reading up on your lecture notes, or using textbooks and the internet to investigate a topic. You may need to interpret data that have been given to you before the session. Alternatively, it may require you to consider your own views on a given subject, and be ready to discuss them. It may just involve deciding the questions on which you particularly want to seek clarification.

**Participation**, by all of the students in the group, is the third pre-requisite for a successful tutorial. You must be prepared to make a personal input into tutorials otherwise sessions will either become a mini lecture or will develop into a dialogue between the tutor and the most vociferous member of the tutorial group.

Speaking up in a tutorial may seem difficult at first, but tutors do appreciate this problem, and you will have the support of your fellow tutees. After all, they are in the same boat, too. Never think that your opinions are worth less than those of anybody else. The best discussions build up in small steps, not as a series of brilliant flashes of inspiration. It is also a good idea to address your remarks to the whole group, rather than just to the tutor. In this way, everybody in the tutorial will become involved.

> **Remember**
>
> *All* participants share responsibility for the successful running of a tutorial. You, as a member of the tutorial group, must be prepared to play your part in making tutorials exciting and effective learning processes.

# 4.3 Learning from laboratory practical classes

Most science subjects are rooted in practical work, and much of our scientific knowledge has been built upon the deductions that scientists have made after analysis of experimental data. Therefore one of the primary objectives of practical classes is to develop a critical awareness of experimental method. Practicals have much more to offer, however. They teach: good laboratory practice, the necessity of paying attention to detail, and an awareness of using technical equipment appropriately. For example, microbiology students learn to handle microbial cultures safely using aseptic technique which, initially, is much more about protecting the cultures from their handlers than it is about protecting students from their cultures! Practicals are also used to demonstrate theories that you will have heard about in lectures. They may provide you with opportunities to exercise your problem-solving skills.

In many practical classes you will be working with a laboratory partner, and in some classes, you may need to form part of a team to tackle problems that are more complex. Acquisition of practical and team-working skills will benefit you enormously in your future career. Above all, safely run practicals are fun.

For each practical class you will almost certainly be given a handout or a workbook that describes the practical work that you will be undertaking and you should make it a golden rule that you *read and understand the introductory material that is provided BEFORE you arrive for a particular class*.

Highlight or underline any important points and make a note of anything you don't understand so that you can ask before you start the experiment. If you make this a habit, you will appreciate why things are done in a particular way and what is going on during the actual class. When recording measurements for representation as a chart, prepare a table and graph paper beforehand so you can easily and neatly note down your data as they are collected, and quickly plot them on a graph. This will enable you to identify anomalous points so that you can repeat them within the practical time allocation. **Note:** it is very good practice to keep a notebook specifically for laboratory work and to enter your data directly into it. This is so that you learn the importance of recording your observations at the time they are made, and is excellent practice for when you are conducting independent investigations. By preparing for the practical in this manner, you will greatly add to your understanding and enjoyment of the practical session.

The most challenging part of an experiment is obtaining a useful set of results. There are several steps to increase the likelihood that your experiment will be successful and these are outlined below.

---

### Checklist for recording data

- Set any equipment appropriately and then make sure you use it correctly throughout the experiment.
- Take accurate and careful readings.
- When taking timed readings – take readings at the <u>exact</u> time required.
- Pre-prepare a results table, preferably in a dedicated laboratory notebook, so that the data can be jotted straight into it. When appropriate, plot results on a graph as you go along – so that you can spot any anomalies and repeat measurements if necessary.

---

## 4.4 Field trips

Field trips allow you to make observations and to collect data in a manner that usually cannot be done in a laboratory. Because they are scientific investigations, all the information in the previous section is relevant; the laboratory notebook is, however, usually called the field notebook.

Results collected on a field trip will be influenced by a variety of external factors that you cannot control and are therefore likely to be more complex than those collected from laboratory-based practical experiments. Dealing with these uncertainties will give you more of an understanding of the issues that can affect scientific investigations. The effects of a host of external factors might require you to think about a topic in a wider context, encouraging you make connections between different areas of a subject. You will then gain a broader overview of the topic.

On a field trip you are likely to be working as part of a team with each group member making different observations. This means that you can assemble a much more comprehensive set of results than each person collecting results individually. Moreover, when teams work well together, the whole experience can be great fun.

Actively collecting data outdoors can be a much more memorable experience than collecting data in your usual practical laboratory so you are likely to remember more of what you actually did and the reasons why. Often, however, the most memorable parts of a field trip are the events that have nothing to do with your investigation, such as your best mate falling into a stream and getting soaked through, and these remain with you the longest!

Field trips are, by their very nature, organized outside the safe confines of a university building, and so all participants must be aware of potential hazards, how to avoid their dangers, and know what to do if things go wrong. So, in order to make a field trip a success, you should make sure that you are properly equipped with the recommended kit, follow any instructions you are given and ALWAYS do as your field trip supervisor(s) instructs. When assembling your kit remember to include:

- appropriate clothing, including long-sleeved shirts and long trousers which offer protection against the sun, stinging and prickly plants and biting and stinging animals. Remember, also, that several thinner layers are better than one or two thick ones.
- appropriate footwear; flip flops and high heels are unsuitable for walking far – Wellington boots are not designed for many country terrains
- relevant equipment, including pens and pencils, paper, field notebook, etc.
- communication equipment, although mobile phones may not work in remote places
- medication for any allergies that you may have
- sunscreen/insect repellent
- backpack and full water bottle

Do not be tempted to take prized possessions that could easily become damaged, such as an expensive digital camera or your favourite pair of trousers; their ruin could spoil your impression of the trip.

Other items such as specialized scientific equipment, first aid kits, compasses and survival gear should be provided by your university department or the field station.

Finally, remember that while you are on your trip you must take only the samples necessary for your work; you should cause minimal disruption that could harm any animals or plants and you must not leave any litter that could damage the environment. As the old saying goes: *"Leave only footprints: take only memories"*.

---

**Checklist for a successful field trip**

- Be aware of potential hazards and how to react in an emergency.
- Take appropriate items of clothing, equipment and medication.
- Comply with any departmental instructions.
- Follow instructions from your trip leader.
- Do not take prized or expensive personal items.
- Respect the environment you visit.

---

# 4.5 Teamwork

Much of this guide is about independent learning, but there are times when you will need to work as part of a team. At its simplest, teamwork involves learning to work effectively with a lab partner, as many practical exercises require that you work in pairs to complete the tasks on time. To be effective, both of you should understand the aim of the experiment and be prepared to contribute equally to the outcome of the practical. It is not unusual to see pairs of students conducting experiments in the lab, where one of the pair is relatively passive and doing very little, while the other is carrying out all the thinking required, as well as performing the bulk of the practical work. Although the passive member of the team appears superficially to benefit from this arrangement, the *most* benefit is derived by the active partner, who has learnt the skills of preparation, organization, time management, use of equipment, and so on. Maximum benefit will, of course, be obtained by both students if both play an active role in preparing for, and participating in, the practical session. The added bonus of following this advice is that you are also likely to find that your practical sessions will tend to go more smoothly and will be completed sooner.

### 4.5.1 Large teams

As well as working in pairs in practical classes, teamwork may also involve larger team exercises. Working as a group, you will typically achieve more than the sum of the individual efforts and so will be able to tackle bigger topics. By drawing on the different strengths of group members, individuals within the team can learn from one another.

All this sounds great but successful groups don't just happen. There are active steps that you can take to ensure the success of any group of which you are a part. Understanding the dynamics of the group is fundamental to this process and there is no magic formula that will work in every situation. This is because each group will comprise individuals each with different skills and personal strengths and weaknesses.

In every group, individual members will have individual responsibilities. Each person will have:

- specific tasks to accomplish on their own which need to be brought back to the group
- a contribution to make to the work done by other members of the group; most often, this is done by **constructive** criticism of the efforts of other team members
- a responsibility to ensure that the team works effectively together

And, within the team, there are three interrelated areas of activity:

- task-related activities, directed to achieving the objective set for the group
- group-related activities, directed to ensuring that the group works together effectively
- individual tasks for group members

Effective groups allow individuals the freedom to achieve their own objectives, thus allowing the group to achieve the overall objective. In the most effective teams, all members are aware of their individual responsibilities, the responsibilities of other members, and the responsibility they owe to the group. Any individual may take on more than one role.

To be effective, every group needs:

- a team leader, or at least someone to co-ordinate the activities of the group. This person is responsible for allocation of tasks and for ensuring that good communications are maintained with all team members. If the final product of the team exercise is written communication, the team leader might, for example, take on the role of editor to ensure a uniformity of written style is imposed.
- good communication with all team members. Every member of the team should be present at team meetings, so these need to be arranged for times when everyone can be present and at a venue that is accessible to all members of the group. Any job inevitably takes longer than envisaged at the outset and deadlines have a nasty habit of creeping up rapidly. So, to avoid unpleasant shocks, don't leave everything to the last minute.
- shared responsibility between all team members for all of the output from the team effort. Just because you are not primarily responsible for a task, this does not mean that you should not help to improve it if it has not been done well, and don't just blame the individual whose primary responsibility it was. Ultimately, who is going to look bad for inferior work produced by your team?
- allocation of tasks according to the specialist talents of *its various members,* although it is important to be flexible in the roles that you take on when engaged in teamwork
- good group dynamics, where team members are supportive towards the others on the team, are unselfish, and do not form cliques within the group

**Consider the following example:** a team has three members who make an average effort and is led by a member who is outstandingly productive. Despite this, however, there is one member of the group who never answers emails, does not turn up for group meetings and has not produced a single piece of work. Clearly it would be unfair for that individual to benefit from the hard work of the others. It is particularly hard on the group leader who is otherwise dynamic and effective.

Sadly, instances like this do occur. Where appropriate assessment is in place, group members would be given the opportunity to penalize team members who do not contribute fully to the work.

---

**Checklist for effective teamwork**

- Good communication – this underpins every successful team.
- Understanding group dynamics – this will help you to make the most of any teamwork in which you engage.
- Recognition and utilization of the different strengths of individual members of the team.
- Team members who fully engage with the task and take their responsibilities seriously.

---

# 4.6 Books

## 4.6.1 Buying books

If your personal study is to be effective, you will require a number of textbooks. School courses tend to work from defined set books but for most university courses you will have greater freedom of choice. Which books should you buy, and from where should you buy them?

## Choosing a book

You will probably be recommended to consider buying a variety of books. One of the first steps that you can take to help you make the decision on what to buy is to talk to last year's students about different texts. Was the coverage insufficient, or was it over-the-top? Was it up-to-date? Was the course designed with that book in mind, or another book, or none at all? Talk to the people who teach on your course, and check that the book you propose to buy is suitable. It is also important to check that you will not be required to work from a particular set text if you decide that you do not want to buy it.

You should also visit the library and spend a little time looking at the array of books that they have on related subjects. Scan them to get a "feel" for the book. You need not attempt to understand the whole content of these books at first. Do you find the text style readable? Are the illustrations clear? Is the text properly sub-divided into sections with appropriate sub-headings, or are you faced with a monotonous sea of print? Does each section have an introduction and a summary of the material it contains? Dip into random paragraphs to see if they are too long. What do you feel about sentence length? It can be very difficult to read long, complex sentences that contain several ideas, but when people are writing texts they may get so caught up in their ideas, which are, of course, so fascinating to them that they forget the poor reader! See what I mean? Ask yourself: "...*would I enjoy working from this book*?"

## Actually purchasing your books

You can either buy new or second-hand books. Many university towns and cities are fortunate in having a number of bookshops, but there is little point in shopping around as the price of books hardly varies between them. Alternatively, it is sometimes possible to purchase books from internet sites at discounted prices. At this point, however, a word of caution is necessary. Some bookshops stock expensive hardback books when cheaper paperback versions are available. The difference in price between a paperback and a hardback book can be significant and so you may end up paying quite a lot extra for a couple of bits of board! It is also a good idea to check that a new edition of the book that you want is not just about to be published.

Students in higher years frequently sell textbooks that they used earlier in their studies, often through advertisements placed on notice boards. Buying books in this way can save considerably on the cost of a brand new textbook. Before buying, however, remember to use the guidelines above to judge whether the text would really suit your purposes. Ask yourself why the book is being sold. You should expect second-hand textbooks to show signs of wear and tear, but if it is sold "as new", was it *really* useful for the course for which it was recommended? Don't buy a second-hand book solely on the recommendation of the seller.

## Before you buy

Check the edition of the book being sold. Some subjects like molecular biology advance at an alarming rate, and at higher levels, a three-year-old text may be hopelessly out of date. By contrast, anatomy books, for example, would not be expected to change at the same rate. If the textbook on offer does not appear to be the latest edition, then be very cautious about buying it. If you have any queries about buying a book, you should consult the person running the course.

# 4.7 Using libraries

Libraries contain tens of thousands of books and journals, and their very size can be daunting when you first visit them. Even students who are used to libraries at school or in their home towns can feel intimidated. Fear not, help is at hand. University libraries are organized to assist you with your studies, and there will be a range of resources to help you with searching, evaluating, managing and referencing information, as well as advising how to keep up to date with new information. They will also be able to advise on copyright and plagiarism issues.

### 4.7.1 Making the most of the library facilities

There are three main reasons why you will use the library: quiet study, consulting or borrowing textbooks, and looking up reference material in journals. Within the libraries are desks and tables that help you study in peace and quiet.

Broadly speaking, there are three types of reading material to be found in academic libraries; textbooks, advanced books on specific academic topics, and journals. In general, textbooks are collected together in different sections of the library by subject and "classmark", and are stored separately from journals.

Many universities make a point of introducing new students to the relevant libraries, showing them where material is kept, how to access it and the various rules of the library. This introductory visit will certainly cover how to find what you are looking for – so pay attention since this advice will prove invaluable later on in your studies!

## Borrowing books – and fines!

Most textbooks and sometimes bound volumes of journals may be borrowed from the university libraries. Most books can be borrowed for extended periods but there are some that are in high demand and may only be borrowed for a limited time to allow others fair access to the material. Books in really high demand are loaned out for just a few hours. This is usually because a book is required for a particular course and so, for a limited period, a large number of students will need access to it. In these situations, the book is transferred to the "counter collection", which means that it is only available on request from the librarian on the counter. This allows all students the opportunity to refer to the book, rather than the lucky individual who happens to borrow it first.

Overdue books and journals attract fines that can quickly build up to significant and alarming sums of money. As well as being potentially expensive, it is bad manners to keep a book longer than necessary, since others may require access to the same text.

If a library book is not available when you first want it, it is sensible to ask for it to be reserved. As well as ensuring that you eventually have access to the book, it also alerts library staff to the demands for that book. This may mean that the library buys additional copies for future use.

## Ask for help

A library can be a daunting place when you first start to use it. When starting out, use the library catalogue (it will be available online) when searching for specific books and journals.

Will you make mistakes?

Will you fail to find references?

Will you need advice on the best way of tackling a particular search?

Yes, Yes, and Yes. Do not despair. The library staff are highly trained and are expert in such matters. They are there to help you, so don't waste hours getting nowhere – ask them for help! They will be pleased to point you in the right direction, and to show you where you have gone wrong. This will help you to avoid those pitfalls next time you need to search for information.

### 4.7.2 *Journal papers and how to understand them*

*There was once a pathologist who would come into his laboratory every Friday morning, hand over the latest copy of a famous medical journal and say to his staff: "Well, here are this week's fairy stories". Although the pathologist was making a joke there is an element of truth about what he said.*

At school or college, textbooks will provide you with all the information that you need to excel in your subject. At university, while you may get an excellent grounding in the subject from textbooks in your first year, you will soon need to start reading, and understanding, scientific papers.

Scientific papers are written in a highly structured, conventional manner. It is important that you appreciate how the conventions work if you are to get the most from the papers, so we need to start by considering how papers are written and published.

A journal is a regular publication (perhaps weekly or monthly) in which academics and researchers will publish their research findings. Each published research study is called a "paper" (in science, it is called a "scientific paper") and is extremely detailed so that the reader can repeat the work if necessary. We will talk more about research papers below. These days, journals are nearly always also available in electronic format and so academics and students can read journals from their computer rather than having to visit the library to do so.

University libraries subscribe to a large number of journals devoted to a staggering array of subjects. Current issues of the journals (i.e. recent issues produced that week or month) will be found on the "current journals" shelves of the library until a volume (usually a complete year's worth of individual issues) is completed. Shortly after the volume has been completed, it will be sent away to be bound as a hardback volume. The "bound journal" is then returned to the library, and is stored alongside earlier volumes of the same journal. The various bound journals are arranged alphabetically by journal title and are also placed in date order as you would expect.

As well as journals being listed in the relevant library catalogue, at the end of each bay are notices saying which journals it contains (e.g. *Nature or The Lancet*). It goes without saying that electronic journals don't disappear for binding!

### 4.7.3 *How scientific papers are published*

Scientific researchers aim to publish the results of their work in high quality journals with a large readership. The work is written up in the form of a "paper" and then submitted for consideration by their preferred journal. These papers are usually sent to two or more referees for "peer review" before they are published. Peer review means that the submitted paper will be reviewed by several other academic experts ("peers") who will be able to comment on the quality of the paper and spot any issues that need to be addressed. Their job is to take a critical view of the material that has been submitted for publication and then to write a report to the editor of the journal, pointing out any matters of concern.

The sorts of questions asked during the peer review process include:

- are the research findings of the author(s) really original?
- do the experimental results described fully support the conclusions drawn by the author(s)?
- is the paper clearly written so as to be unambiguous?
- is the paper comprehensive so that the experiments can be repeated by the reader to test their validity?

...and so on...

Only if a paper meets these criteria will it be published in a peer-reviewed journal.

This thorough approach generally works well, but the system is not perfect and mistakes do creep into the literature.

There are three major types of paper: full original research papers (often collectively called the "primary literature"), short "research letters", and review articles. These are now considered in turn.

## Primary literature

Most of the papers that you will come across are full descriptions of original experiments made directly by researchers. Although the details differ between journals, a typical scientific paper includes:

- abstract – a very brief summary of the work, the major results, and the author's conclusions
- introduction – a short overview of that specific field of research and where this new research fits in
- materials and methods – a concise description of the methods used to undertake the research
- results – a detailed presentation of the original experimental results; depending on the experiments, this section may also include statistical analysis (see *Catch Up Maths & Stats* for details on why authors use particular statistical tests to analyse their data)
- discussion – a description as to what the author concludes that these data show
- references – a list of the other research papers that the author refers to in his work (allowing a reader to look further into particular aspects of the topic)

## Research letters

When results, sometimes only from single experiments, are too important to wait for the whole body of work to be completed before publication, then these smaller sets of results may be released as research letters.

Alternatively, a research letter may be a critique of work that has already been published, perhaps including data to refute the previous paper. In such cases, the author(s) of the original work are often invited to publish a reply, most often appearing next to the first research letter.

## Review articles

Given the very high volume of research papers published, it would be a huge task for a student to read all the relevant papers in a subject area. This is when review articles can be helpful, particularly when finding your way around an unfamiliar area. Therefore, although we have described reviews last in the discussion of the three types of journal, they should often be the first place you start when learning about a new subject area.

Reviews are typically written by experts in their field and give either an in-depth view of a particular topic or present a broad overview of their field of interest. Reviews cite many primary publications (papers describing original research) in support of their arguments, and interested readers can use these to explore the literature further, often with the benefit of critical comments made in the review.

A variant of the review article is the short "news and views" type article, often devoted to a critical review of a specific paper published in the same edition of the journal. "News and views" articles tend to be commissioned by the journal from leading experts in the field.

### 4.7.4  How should you read a scientific paper?

How you read a scientific paper (i.e. a paper from the primary literature – see above) depends on what you want to do with the information. Early in your undergraduate career, you should aim to get a feel for what is being published in an area. However, by the time you undertake a research project in your final year, particularly if it involves experimental work, you will need to pay much more attention to the way the science was done.

A good approach to take when faced with reading a scientific paper is to go through it in the order of the steps listed below.

**Step 1**
Look at the title which is a crucial part of any paper. As many papers may be published on a topic, authors often try to make their titles interesting, to encourage the reader to explore further: "*GM foods – a case of resistance*" is an allusion both to the antibiotic resistance markers left in first-generation insect-resistant plants and to the public opposition in the UK to the introduction of GM plants into commercial agriculture. If you come to write papers, you will need to remember that the title may be the only part of the paper that many people will read.

**Step 2**
Read the abstract or summary. This is a short description of the principal findings of the paper, and, together with the title, gives the reader a feel for the subject. For many, reading the abstract will be sufficient, but if this is all you read you may miss out on important details that lie hidden in the body of the text. It is not always wise to rely absolutely on the authors of a paper to highlight in the abstract what is important and "hidden gems" may be found by those who are prepared to explore deeper into papers.

**Step 3**

What you read next depends on why you are reading the paper and what you want to do with the information. For someone who is relatively unfamiliar with the research in that area it may be invaluable to read the introduction section next since this sets out the background against which the research was carried out and introduces the topic in context. People already familiar with similar work may not find the introduction of much interest and might skip this step.

**Step 4**

The next step is to read the results that are reported in the paper and the interpretation placed on them by the authors in the discussion section. Typically, "Results" and "Discussion" sections are written separately, but when complex sets of experiments are being reported, particularly if the implications of one set of results need to be explained before the next set can be understood, a combined "Results and discussion" section may be provided.

**Step 5**

The papers to which the author(s) refer are described in the reference list and you might want to follow up the information in the paper by reading some of these, especially if you are preparing a dissertation or literature review. Finally, the acknowledgements section of the paper is typically very short and often need not be read by the students. However, it contains important information, particularly concerning the way that the work was funded.

**Step 6**

If you wish to do similar work to that described in the paper, you will need to read the "Materials and methods" section. In places, the "Materials and methods" section may not describe a particular method used in any detail, but instead refer to other papers in which this is described.

# 4.8  Using the internet as a source of information

Although it now seems almost inconceivable, not many years ago, the only way to follow scientific progress was by reading the published journal papers in libraries. The advent of powerful and widely accessible computing and the existence of electronic journals has changed all that, for the better. Now, locating the journal articles you need to read and then reading them is fast and easy, if you know how!

When you need to search the primary scientific literature, a number of online tools can help. It is important that you learn to use them as they will undoubtedly make your information searches quicker and easier. Three particularly helpful tools are:

- Web of Science (http://isiwebofknowledge.com/) – the Web of Knowledge covers a total of 23 000 journals but allows users just to access the relevant scientific articles via Web of Science. Coverage does, however, get patchy, the further back in time you need to search

- PubMed (www.ncbi.nlm.nih.gov/pubmed/) – this is a service of the US National Library of Medicine that includes over 18 million citations from Medline and other life science journals for biomedical articles back to 1948. PubMed includes links to full text articles and other related resources
- Google Scholar (http://scholar.google.co.uk/) – provides users with the opportunity to use a range of search options across the scientific and medical literature

These three database "search engines" allow users to search for work published in journals using key words, authors, journal title, etc. In addition, most search engines like these now allow you to click on links in the reference sections of papers and you will be taken to the full text of that article too, allowing you to build a web around the original paper by following links forwards and backwards.

None of these tools is difficult to use, and they can prove invaluable, particularly during project work. When you first use these databases, it is easy to get overwhelmed by the number of citations that you find. All of these databases do, however, allow you to refine your search, narrowing down the list of papers, perhaps to just the one that you need. You may do this by combining different keywords, author names, journals, year of publication or any combination of these, providing, of course, that you have this information to hand.

Coverage of the literature is constantly being updated, so you will find new papers almost as soon as they are published. Indeed, with some journals, you may have access to the electronic version of an article before its paper version appears from the printing presses. The coverage of older papers is variable, depending on the database, but for most there is now reasonable coverage of journals published from the 1960s to the present day. Many of these databases are undergoing frequent redesigns so we have not provided detailed advice on their use – it is all fairly intuitive.

Assuming that your university library subscribes to the journal containing the article found by your search, then you will be able to have free access, from your computer, to the full article, so there is no need to go hunting through the library to find the paper copy. If your library does not subscribe to the journal (although most university libraries do subscribe to a huge number, there will be some to which it does not), then you will still be shown the title and abstract and offered the chance to buy an electronic copy. Before you buy, check the abstract to see if it really is a paper you need and then talk to the librarian to see if there is a cheaper way to gain access.

There are a number of other similar tools, which you are free to explore and your librarians will give you advice on how to get the most from them.

**Remember**

Databases are only as good as the data that they contain and they don't all cover all of the journals. It is advisable to use more than one resource when researching topics.

## 4.8.1 Finding reliable internet resources

This brings up the whole question of how reliable the internet is as a source of information. It is **essential** to remember that it is very easy to post information on the web and many people do. The reasons people put up information are many and various; not all of them are for the greater good. Even apparently reputable websites may be designed to give a particular "spin" to a topic.

You need to be very very careful when evaluating information from the internet, particularly about the **structure and content** of the material and also what **authority** the website has. Except for web pages in academic journals (which includes papers identified by the Web of Science, Medline, PubMed, etc.) other web pages are rarely "peer-reviewed". That means that it is down to you, the student, to evaluate which web pages to trust, and which to reject. The questions asked during the process of peer review (see above) may help you to make the right judgements. Here are some further questions to help decide:

- is the information relevant and pitched at the right level?
- are fact and fiction clearly differentiated?
- are references provided?
- are there links to independent sites in support of the content of the site in question?
- has the information been validated in any way?
- is the site up-to-date?

Sites that are not supported by valid references or external links or those that are not substantiated by peer review are more likely to be inaccurate and/or biased.

When it comes to considering the authority of a website, you may also like to bear the following in mind. A website produced by a corporation (with a web address ending in ".co" or ".com") may give a view that favours that company. After all, companies exist to sell their products. In contrast, university sites in the UK contain ".ac.uk" and in the USA they end in ".edu". UK government sites contain ".gov" or ".org".

However, just because a website is not a company site does not guarantee reliability of the information. You should consider:

- who wrote the material?
- why was it written?
- are the credentials/qualifications of the author shown and relevant?
- is the site associated with a reputable institution (universities/research institutes/professional associations/government bodies)?
- can you see contact details for correspondence?

## Wikipedia

In their early years at university, many students use Wikipedia as a source of information. For those of you who have not encountered Wikipedia yet, this is a dynamic, online encyclopaedia that anyone can edit. It contains many good pages which have external references and these are a useful resource. It claims to have a neutral viewpoint, its content is free and it has a code of conduct, part of which states that Wikipedia has no firm rules. You should, however, be **very careful** how you use Wikipedia. Although it is a good secondary source of information and as such will provide background information on a huge array of topics, it should not be quoted as a primary reference because it is not peer-reviewed and anyone can edit its pages, leaving open the possibility of unreliable information being posted on it.

Looking at the "discussion" tag may give some idea of how reliable the information is on any given page, particularly if it concerns a controversial topic. Furthermore, information may change after you have read a page so any reference you quote may change and others will not be able to access the information you cited. This means you need to take care to provide a **full** reference to the **actual page** you accessed. These may be traced using the "history" tag. Here is an example of how to do this:

WIKIPEDIA. 2009. *Charles Darwin* [online]. [Accessed 20:30 hrs Monday 26th January 2009]. Available from http://en.wikipedia.org/w/index.php?title=Charles_Darwin&oldid=265888987. 2009. The link to the current, live page is simply: http://en.wikipedia.org/wiki/Charles_Darwin.

Even if you can satisfy yourself that the website looks fine, remember that, just occasionally, science undergoes seismic changes.

In 1978 Peter Mitchell was awarded the Nobel Prize in Chemistry for expounding the chemiosmotic hypothesis to explain how mitochondria generate ATP. A few years previously he was not at all well regarded by some scientists in his field. Suppose he had had a website with the same content before and after he won his prize. How do you think that these would differ? How do you think your views would have changed on what you read?

# Chapter 5  Presenting your work

## 5.1  Plagiarism

Material obtained from textbooks and scientific papers will, in many cases, form the basis of a considerable part of your work. You **must** acknowledge the work of the original authors with a citation and a reference, so that your reader knows the source of your information and can check it. Plagiarism is defined as presenting someone else's work as your own. Here, work means any intellectual output and typically includes text, data and images. You may often be asked to provide an electronic copy of an assignment so that it can be assessed for originality by software designed to detect plagiarism.

Here are two examples of using a source text: one illustrating plagiarism; the other showing creative thought. These are presented together with the extract that was used as the source. Version 1 is from page 4 of an article: *"The Future of Genetically Modified Crops: Lessons from the Green Revolution"*, by Felicia Wu and William P. Butz, also at http://www.rand.org/pubs/monographs/2004/RAND_MG161.pdf [accessed 22/1/09].

### Version 1 – the original paper

*"It is in the context of the hundred-year history of technological change that we consider the most recent movement in world agriculture: genetically modified (GM) crops, produced through modern biotechnology that enables genes to be transferred across different species and even across different plant kingdoms, to introduce desired traits into a host plant. After just a decade, the GM crop movement is already beginning to revolutionize agriculture in new ways, with previously unachievable benefits and novel potential risks.*

*The study of GM crops focuses on the genetically modified crop movement and whether it has the potential to revolutionize agriculture in the developing world and to truly become the "Gene Revolution" that some of its proponents already call it. We focus on the developing world because it is in greatest need of a new agricultural revolution – whether in the form of GM crops or another revolution altogether – given the rapidly growing populations, lagging agricultural technologies and malnutrition in the world's poorest nations.*

*Three presumptions motivated this study: (1) reducing hunger and malnutrition is desirable; (2) now, as in the past, revolutionary technological change in world agriculture can substantially reduce hunger and malnutrition; and (3) now, as in the past, agricultural technologies can be designed and used such that the majority of farmers, consumers, and experts will agree that the technologies are worth their attendant risks."*

## Version 2

*"This report considers the most recent movement in world agriculture within the context of the hundred-year history of technological change. Genetically modified (GM) crops, produced through modern biotechnology, enable genes to be transferred between different species and even different plant kingdoms, so that desired traits into a host plant are introduced. It has only taken little more than a decade for the GM crop movement to revolutionize agriculture in new ways, and although there are now many previously unachievable benefits, these have been accompanied by novel potential risks. The report will focus on whether these new technologies have the potential to revolutionize agriculture, particularly in the developing world, thereby becoming the "Gene Revolution" in contrast to the "Green Revolution" that took place in the mid-twentieth century when the introduction of intensive use of agrochemicals, selective breeding and improved agricultural management, boosted production. There will be particular focus on the developing world – the world's poorest nations – because it has greatest need of a new agricultural revolution to try to avoid disaster for the rapidly growing populations which are under threat of malnutrition due to backward agricultural technologies."*

## Version 3

*"Since the early 1900s, an increasing number of innovations and developments in agricultural technologies have led to massive increases in crop production. The introduction of intensive use of agrochemicals, selective breeding and improved agricultural management, in the mid-1900s, boosted production and created what is now dubbed the "Green Revolution". The next great advance is now coming through improvements in the ability to manipulate the genetic material directly, and during the past ten years these scientific techniques have opened the way for the successful transfer of specific desired phenotypic traits not only between many different species, but also extending between different plant kingdoms to produce genetically modified (GM) crops. This progress has been likened to a "Gene Revolution"! However, any perceived benefits of GM crops are accompanied by real potential risks, and the cost–benefit debate must take place to ensure that these new technologies do not create further problems for the future.*

*Parts of the world that are in most need of agricultural improvements are centred in the poorest nations, where, typically, underdeveloped agricultural technology is unable to cope with the increasing population, resulting in widespread hunger and malnutrition. This report will, therefore, focus on the potential benefits that the new GM crops might bring to these Third World regions and investigate the methods by which any accompanying risks can be limited."*

Version 1 is the original text. Version 2 shows several changes, mainly with different words being inserted but with some original additions. It is not sufficiently different from the original to avoid the accusation of plagiarism. In only one place, when the "Green Revolution" is mentioned, does it show any original thought. Thus, it is considered to be plagiarized from the first version, even if a reference to the original text had been included. Version 3 shows independent thought, does not use the same sentences or phrases, except when describing common terms (the "Green Revolution", the "Third World" etc.), presents several points in a different order and makes connections to other ideas to explain the context of the topic. This would still need to include a reference to the original paper since this is where some of the ideas originated (but were not copied verbatim).

### AVOID PLAGIARISM

It is never a good idea to copy out large sections from a textbook or other source. Apart from the fact that this is plagiarism, you will derive very little educational benefit from such an exercise. You may also get caught, and you will be heavily penalized. In the most extreme cases you may be expelled from your university. As work is routinely submitted to a plagiarism detection service, there is a very high chance that, should you be tempted to pass off the work of others as your own, you will be caught. It is far better to show how you can relate ideas to one another. At university, it is this higher level of understanding that we are trying to develop.

# 5.2  Good writing and writing style

The ability to present information effectively is a skill that will be useful throughout your life, and efficient communication is essential if you work within a team. At university you will be required to write essays, practical reports and projects, to give presentations as talks and possibly as posters. Many of these require common skills, albeit tailored to the specific task. These include planning, preparation, organization and an understanding of your audience. The way that you present not only reflects what you know about a subject, it can also show how well you can analyse a topic and integrate it with other areas of thought or knowledge. A recurring theme present in all types of good presentation is the organization of the material, where material is grouped into a beginning, a middle, and an end.

Lewis Carroll summed up the process in *"Alice's Adventures in Wonderland"*:

> *The White Rabbit put on his spectacles. "Where shall I begin, please your Majesty?" he asked.*
> *"Begin at the beginning," the King said, very gravely, "and go on till you come to the end: then stop."*

The manner in which material appears on the page, or screen, can also significantly affect how it is received, and advice is included in the *Appendices* on how you can use your computer to help you present your work in the most appropriate and interesting way.

## 5.2.1  *Third person, passive voice and the past tense*

Whatever you have been told at school or college, your writing at university level will sound more authoritative and objective when written in the "third person".

Instead of writing "*In this essay I will describe...*" it is better to write "*This essay describes...*". This is particularly important if you have been invited to write critically about a subject since you need to draw unbiased conclusions in such essays.

Many writers, especially those in scientific disciplines, write in the **passive voice**, as in the following example: "These organisms were classified by Margulis". However, excessive use of the passive voice leads to reader fatigue and a dull and lifeless text. To make it read better, a mix of passive and active voices should be used, as in the example: "After Margulis had completed his classification of organisms, the research was continued by Schmidt".

Write practical/laboratory reports in the past tense. This is particularly important in sections on methodology, as if you use the present tense, e.g. "the grollifying cordwanglers are added at this point", it sounds like a recipe.

### 5.2.2 *Sentences*

#### *Verbs and nouns*

Every complete sentence MUST have a verb – an 'action' word. The simplest sentence contains a single word of command. An example would be "Go!". Generally, however, sentences comprise at least a noun and a verb. "John laughed" or "Pigs fly" are examples of very short sentences. The verbs, "laughed" and "fly", are action words. In these cases, the noun, "John", is a proper noun – it is the name of something (John) – and so its first letter is written using an upper-case character regardless of where it comes in the sentence. Ordinary nouns, such as "pigs" don't get such special treatment unless they start a sentence.

#### *Subjects and objects*

In the sentences above, "John" and "pigs" are also the "subjects". Occasionally, the verb is referred to as the predicate of the subject, since it tells you something about the subject. Most sentences also have an object; this completes the meaning of the verb. The "object" in the sentence "John laughed at the joke" is "joke" and in "Pigs fly home" it is "home".

#### *Pronouns*

Sometimes pronouns are used in place of nouns, for example, I, you, he, she, it, we, you, they, yours, mine, this, that, some, none, and so on. "John laughed at the joke" could be written "He laughed at it", where "he" and "it" are pronouns. Pronouns change, depending on the context in which they are used. When it is the subject of the sentence, "I" is the correct personal pronoun but when "I" becomes the object of the sentence, it changes to "me", for example, "I laughed at the joke", but "John laughed at me".

One area where this causes major confusion is in the use of "who" and "whom". In the sentence "Who is there?", "who" is the subject; "with whom you have spoken" is a phrase where "whom" is used, correctly, as the object of the sentence. Nevertheless, it sounds a bit contrived and it is doubtful whether these days you would hear the latter phrase often spoken. The grammar checking facility in *Microsoft Word* often confuses the use of "who" and "whom".

## Adjectives and adverbs

Adjectives describe nouns; adverbs do the same for verbs and together they make sentences far more interesting and explanatory. In the sentence "Aerodynamic pigs fly acrobatically home" there is one adjective "aerodynamic" and one adverb "acrobatically", whereas the sentence "Jovial John laughed merrily at the funny joke" contains two adjectives, "jovial" and "funny" and one adverb, "merrily".

## Prepositions

Prepositions are words that link nouns, pronouns and phrases to other parts of a sentence. These are the small words, like "in", "at", "under", "on" and so on. The preposition "in" is used in the following sentence "Jovial John laughed merrily at the funny joke in the book" and for the sentence "Aerodynamic pigs fly acrobatically home at bath time", the preposition is "at".

Some grammar 'experts' frown on the idea of ending a sentence with a preposition. Trying to adapt sentences to avoid doing so can sometimes lead to nonsense, as Winston Churchill is said to have remarked to an editor who had clumsily rearranged his prose, *"This is the sort of English up with which I will not put"*[1]. Common usage often means that your sentences do not read too badly if you do end them with a preposition, but it is usually possible to rearrange your sentence so that everything is grammatically correct. Using Winston Churchill's example you could write "I will not put up with this sort of English".

## Conjunctions and interjections

Conjunctions join different parts of sentences together; "and" and "but" are good examples, as are "or", "nor", "if", "when", "whereas" and "because". Our two example sentences actually consist of two separate ideas which can be joined by a "because" and "when" respectively:

"Jovial John laughed merrily *because* there was a funny joke in the book"
"Aerodynamic pigs fly acrobatically home *when* it is bath time"

Interjections such as 'Ah!' or 'Oh dear!' are added to a sentence to heighten the dramatic impact and are often accompanied by exclamation marks! You can use these too liberally! Then your reader may end up feeling as though you are shouting! They should generally be restricted to the spoken word.

## Split infinitives

Returning to a consideration of verbs, some people with a classical education will tell you that it is "wrong to split an infinitive". The infinitive form of any verb is "to [the verb]". The most famous split infinitive is "...*to boldly go*...", where the adverb "boldly" splits the infinitive form of the verb "to go". Although this construction is

---

1  Sir Ernest Gowers' *Plain Words* (1948)

not actually wrong, a sufficient number of people feel that is a very inelegant way of expressing oneself. For that reason alone, it is best avoided whenever possible.

### 5.2.3 Clarity

This means using plain, simple words where plain simple words will do. Simple sentences and simple paragraphs also help with clarity of style.

In general, it is preferable to use short sentences but, if you write longer ones, join phrases together with conjunctions; semicolons are also useful. The previous sentence is an example of how long sentences can be compiled. Paragraphs should be given over to one idea, and have an introductory sentence and a concluding remark.

Read the two paragraphs below. They illustrate what clarity *ought* to be about, even if they only show what does **NOT** constitute good style.

> *Simple sentences contain only one idea. They avoid multiple subordinate phrases. Simplicity can be overdone. Constant use of simple sentences tires the reader. Use of too many simple sentences introduces ideas too rapidly.*
>
> *Alternatively, if authors want to impress their audience, particularly if they have literary pretensions, they may exhibit a desire to show off their expertise at constructing complex word orders, with the effect that by the time the reader has finally and terminally managed to sort out the point of the sentence, then they have forgotten what the beginning of the proclamation was about, and will need to re-read the beginning of the sentence to remind themselves.*

You should avoid paragraphs that comprise a single sentence!

To achieve clarity of style, you should try to avoid:

- unnecessary phrases that add words to your argument but not content, such as "in addition to" where "also" will do
- tautology, defined in the *Oxford English Dictionary* as: "the repetition (esp. in the immediate context) of the same word or phrase, or of the same idea or statement in other words: usually as a fault of style". Examples include "to encode for" or "reiterate again". The first may be expressed as "to encode" or as "to code for". In the second example, the word "again" is unnecessary
- inclusion of words such as "...clearly..." or "...obviously...". What may be clear or obvious to you may not be clear or obvious to your readers; the last thing you want to do is make your readers feel stupid

### 5.2.4 Accepted usage and jargon

Accepted usage means that grammatical constructions that were unacceptable in the past become so prevalent that (almost) everyone now wonders what all the fuss was about. Sentences that end in a preposition ('about'), like the last one, are a good example. A grammatically correct form, acceptable to purists, would be "...become so prevalent that, about what, everyone wonders, was all the fuss"!

Laboratory jargon also sometimes seeps into English usage. A fine example of seepage is the term "sequencing". The *Oxford English Dictionary* definition is "to arrange [objects] in a definite sequence or order". In relation to nucleic acids, however, (almost) everyone now talks of "sequencing" when talking about discovering the order in which nucleotides are already arranged.

### 5.2.5 *Over-use of adjectives*

This can also lead to a lack of clarity when they are piled up before the noun to which they refer. Sometimes these have the force of accepted use, such as the bacteriological term "*extended-spectrum β-lactamases*". However, on other occasions this practice can be misleading. Does "*muscle wasting treatment*" mean a treatment that causes or cures muscle wasting? Appropriate use of a hyphen can help: "*muscle-wasting treatment*" but why not be unambiguous and, instead, state "*treatments for muscle wasting*"?

> **Remember**
>
> Clarity and precision of communication aid critical thinking about the subjects being communicated, so the words you use must communicate what you mean to convey.

### 5.2.6 *Legibility and quality of presentation*

These are undoubtedly of considerable importance in helping students obtain high marks. Coursework these days is usually word-processed, but legibility is essential for essay-style examinations. Legibility is important not because markers deliberately deduct marks for poor presentation or legibility, but because it is much easier to follow an argument if you are not continually being distracted by attempts to translate the hieroglyphics. If you submit word-processed work, as most coursework will be, always use *at least* 1.5 line-spacing. Use double spacing if instructed so to do. This permits written comments to be added to your work.

### 5.2.7 *Waffle and irrelevant material*

Waffle is the repetition of a topic over and over again in slightly different ways, without any new information being presented, thereby destroying the continuity of your argument. It is head of the hate list for all markers faced with a pile of essays or practical reports and should be avoided at all costs. It is much better to be concise, but try not to be too blunt.

Inclusion of irrelevant material is a common fault and occurs when students write about a topic they *would have liked* to write about and that was *nearly* the same as the topic they were actually set. If, for example, you are asked to write an essay on frogs, you will not get any marks for writing an essay about toads just because you have just finished reading "*Wind in the Willows*". Frogs and toads are quite different.

## 5.2.8 Check your writing style

To see how effective your beautiful prose actually is, read it aloud. This will tell you if the text "flows". If it doesn't, check that you have included a subject, a verb and an object in every sentence. Alternatively, see whether you are using punctuation appropriately. Reading aloud will enable you to see where punctuation marks *ought* to be placed.

Correct use of basic grammar includes the following:

- The appropriate use of commas, to indicate a short break in your reading. You should not use commas to join together ideas that are unrelated grammatically.
- The adoption of semi-colons to indicate a longer break; these are useful where related topics are contained within a sentence and their relationship could otherwise be joined by "but" or "and". Typically, the semi-colon is used to separate a main clause from one of lesser importance. A colon is used to separate a clause of text from a list.
- The use of full stops to indicate a significant break.

The following paragraph illustrates appropriate usage of commas, semi-colons, colons and full stops.

> The human body can gain or lose heat from its environment by four physical means: conduction, convection, radiation and evaporation. Normal cellular activity is possible only within a relatively constant temperature range; above this, proteins become irreversibly denatured, resulting in the deterioration in nerve and metabolic function. Temperatures much below the range result in a fatal slowing of metabolism.

## 5.2.9 Some common errors of English usage

Take care with "it's" and "its". "It's" is a contraction of "it is", as in "It's incorrect to use contractions in formal text". Do not use an apostrophe when the meaning is "of it" (as in "belonging to"), for example "...botulinum toxin is a neurotoxin: its main effects are....".

> ...*it is* possible that a mammal may survive...
> may become:
> ...*It's* possible that a mammal may survive...

Note that this form of contraction is usually inappropriate in scientific material.

Other than in the contractions mentioned above, the apostrophe is solely used to form possessives. For example, "the density of cells" may also be written "the cells' density, but not "the cell's density" or "the cells's density".

Apostrophes are never used in plurals, or "plural's" as some would incorrectly say.

While on the subject of apostrophes, in British usage dates do not have apostrophes, as in "*Roger Bannister broke the four-minute mile record in the 1950s*". Be aware, however, that Americans do like the apostrophe "*Neil Armstrong walked on the Moon in the 1960's*" but you should avoid the temptation to follow this example unless you are writing specifically for an American audience.

- The sharp-eyed among you may have noticed the **use of the hyphen** in the paragraph above and near the start of this sentence. A hyphen is used to form a "compound adjective", where two words are used to describe something. No hyphen is needed when words are used together as a noun phrase. An example is "*Charles Darwin was a nineteenth-century naturalist*" has a hyphen, but "*Charles Darwin was a naturalist working in the nineteenth century*" does not.

- Be aware of the difference between **abbreviations and contractions.** "*Prof.*" is an abbreviation of "*Prof*essor" and to indicate this, it is followed by a full stop. In contrast, "*Dr*" is a contraction of "*Doctor*" (the first and last letters are the same as the full word) and as such does not require a full stop.

- **Drug names do not begin with a capital** letter unless they are trade names, for example – "androstenediol" is a drug, "Bolandiol" is a trade name.

- The word **"data"** is the plural of **"datum"**; hence, you should use "data are...." rather than "data is....". Other plural words are: bacteria (singular: bacterium), media (singular: medium), criteria (singular: criterion), phenomena (singular: phenomenon).

- **Do not confuse "dependent" with "dependant"**: the former is an adjective, the latter a noun. So, responses are "concentration-dependent", not "dependant". A dependant is someone who depends on someone else; young children are their parents' dependants.

- **Do not confuse "affect" with "effect"**: either can be used as a noun; either can be used as a verb. Each meaning is distinct. "To affect" as a verb is to aspire to or to cause something to happen, to pretend to. The noun "affect" is a term psychologists use to describe a feeling. In contrast, "to effect" is to bring about or to accomplish and an "effect" is the result of an action.

- **Do not confuse "uninterested" with "disinterested"**: increasingly, people are using "disinterested" to imply lack of concern or indifference. The correct word here is "uninterested"; "disinterested" means not influenced by interests, as in a disinterested third party.

- **Do not confuse "imply" and "infer"**: the former means to suggest something whereas the latter means to conclude or make a deduction from something. So, a set of results may imply that a process is occurring and you can infer from these data that the process is occurring.

- **Be aware of homophones** – words that sound the same but mean different things, like "there" "their", and "they're" (they are), "two", "to" and "too", and "great" and "grate". A biological example is "weather", "whether" and "wether" (a castrated ram).

- Errors are often seen in the **use of "lead"**: "lead" is the present tense of the verb, whereas the past tense is "led". "Lead" as a noun, however, is the chemical element (chemical symbol, Pb) or, possibly, the strip of leather used to stop your dog from escaping.

- **Latin words or phrases should be in italics,** as in "Experiments performed *in vivo* led to different conclusions from those indicated by *in vitro* experiments". (Note the use of "led".) This rule does not apply to abbreviations such as e.g. (*exampli gratia* – for example) and i.e. (*id est* – that is).

- **Names of species.** These should be in italics. The genus name (first word) should have a capital letter but the species name (second word) should not, and you may abbreviate the first letter after the first inclusion. For example, *Homo sapiens*: this can thereafter be written as *H. sapiens*. Care must be taken to avoid confusion when more than one genus name may share a single letter abbreviation.

- **Some words are frequently misspelled**: occurred, protein, receive, noradrenaline, albumin, penicillin, parallel, pipette are common examples.

- Remember that **even spellcheckers can be fooled.** The one that comes with *Microsoft Word* does not like "*noradrenaline*", which, because it is an American program, it would suggest is written as "*noradrenalin*". From the section above, *Word* doesn't like "botulinum", "androstenediol", "Bolandiol", "Pb" and "est", either. These would appear as "outline", "no suggestion", "Boabdil", "Pub" and "set", if you were to accept some of the suggestions *Word* makes!

### 5.2.10 *Some general points of style and punctuation using a word processor*

- Punctuation marks such as commas, full stops, semi-colons, etc. should follow the preceding word without a space.

- There should be no spaces between brackets and the words that they contain.

- Paragraphs should typically follow the modern office style, as in this text. Start a new paragraph at the beginning of the line (do not tab or indent). Leave a blank line between paragraphs. Do not start a new line for a new sentence unless the break is natural; that is, the previous sentence finishes at the end of the previous line. Only press the return key when you want to start a new paragraph.

- Be aware of 'non-breaking' spaces. They should be used when you want to prevent breaks round a line, for example, in references or for initials and names. It is especially useful when using Latin binomials such as *E. coli* where the genus name is nearly always assumed. Press Ctrl-Shift and the spacebar to achieve this in *Microsoft Word*.

## 5.3 Illustrations and tables of data

Illustrative material is very helpful in conveying messages succinctly and it has been said that a picture is worth a thousand words. It would not, however, be sensible to try submitting one picture in place of the one thousand words that you may have been asked to write as part of your in-course assessment!

Contrary to what you may have been told previously, figures and tables act as very useful adjuncts to scientific essays. Figures and tables can make difficult concepts seem simple or can summarize material very economically and so a few well-chosen figures or tables will add considerable value to your essays. Some points to remember about illustrations are:

- do not duplicate the same information by including it in a table and a graph
- number each figure or table in your essay so that you can refer to it at the appropriate point in the text
- give your figures and/or tables a title which is meaningful and indicates why you have included the information
- include a key to define any symbols or abbreviations, or a further short section of description unless the figure is very simple
- provide a reference to the source of the material unless you generated the data for a table or constructed the figure yourself

Remember that including illustrations or photographs in a document will often increase the file size significantly. Sometimes, it may make the document so large that it cannot be sent as an email attachment or, in some cases, stored on portable storage devices. Advice on reducing the size of illustrations and how to insert them into your *Word* document is given in *Appendix A, Section 3.6.*

# 5.4  Referencing your work

At Level 1, a reference list may comprise a simple list of source material that you have consulted when preparing your essay. At higher levels, you will need to be more extensive in your use of references so that by Level 3 your essays and reports should resemble material in the peer-reviewed scientific literature. You should take care with your reference section, as incorrect or inaccurate referencing in essays is penalized. This includes omission of references either from the body of the text or from the reference list, inaccurate citation of papers, and also the inclusion of references that have not been cited in the text.

A good reference list starts when you begin searching the literature relating to your research topic. Much of your literature searching will involve the use of one of a number of bibliographic databases, such as "Web of Science" or "Medline". Each has advantages and disadvantages but whichever tool you choose to find your references, it is important that you keep accurate records of the references that you find *at the time that you use them*, so that you and others may refer to them later. It can be very difficult, and frustrating, trying to track down papers later on. Remember, also, that the web is an ephemeral source of information. This can be a particular problem with pages from Wikipedia, the free online encyclopaedia, where anyone can edit a page at any time. Keeping track of changes can be difficult. It is sensible to keep a copy of the information that you access on the web. This may be either electronically or as a print copy.

When compiling your own reference lists for major documents, it may be useful to consider using specialized reference management software such as *EndNote*.

### 5.4.1 *What information is included in a reference?*

You may find lists of "References" at the end of book chapters that contain references to all the papers referred to in the text. Alternatively, lists of "Additional reading" may be given; these lists are usually not papers actually cited in the text but are more general review-type articles that the authors consider useful further reading. In either case, the individual reference may look something like:

> Watson, J.D. & Crick, F.H.C. (1953) MOLECULAR STRUCTURE OF NUCLEIC ACIDS: A Structure for Deoxyribonucleic Acid. *Nature*, *171* (4356): *737–738.*

The precise way in which a reference is cited can vary considerably, but they all tend to conform to a general pattern. In the example above, the first item is the authors' names. In this case, the paper was written by two authors (Watson, J.D. & Crick, F.H.C) – their names may be familiar. In papers with several authors, sometimes only the first author's name is given followed by "*et al.*" short for *et alii*, meaning "and others".

Next is written the year of publication (1953), in this case given in full and in brackets, and this is followed by the title of the paper (MOLECULAR STRUCTURE OF NUCLEIC ACIDS: A Structure for Deoxyribonucleic Acid). After this comes the name of the journal in which the paper appears (in this case, *Nature*). This is sometimes given in full but is usually abbreviated. Some abbreviations can be fairly obscure, although a knowledge of the subject matter may provide clues to the full title of the journal. There is no single standard for the abbreviation of journal names but if you are in any doubt, you would be wise to conform to abbreviations used by the Institute for Scientific Information, and referred to by the Web of Science. Journal and book titles conventionally appear in italics.

The series of numbers (*171* (*4356*): *737–738*) following the journal name indicate, in order; the volume in which the paper appears, in this case volume 171; the issue number in the volume that carries the paper "(4356)" – this is frequently omitted from reference lists; and finally, the first and last pages of the paper (737–738). In this case, the paper is very short, but nonetheless significant. This just proves that it is true that size doesn't matter.

The example above shows a fairly full reference. This is a most useful form of reference presentation because the more information you have about a reference, the easier it is to find, even if a mistake, such as the transposition of numbers, is introduced. For some purposes, a reference may only comprise a journal title, volume number, and a reference to the first page of the paper. Such references can prove impossible to trace if a mistake creeps into the citation.

### 5.4.2 *Styles of referencing*

Many universities recommend the use of the "Harvard" style for referencing material and this is the one that is used most commonly to cite references in academic works. The Harvard style uses author and year of publication in brackets in the text, and then the full reference details in the reference list.

Despite its name, the Harvard style does not fall under the jurisdiction of any single institution. Consequently, there is no authority that maintains the rules of this style and variations have evolved over time with different people having different ideas of what constitutes **the** Harvard style. So…

> *…it is essential that you follow precisely the instructions given on referencing for EVERY piece of work that you submit.*

*EndNote*, a commercially available bibliographic software package, has over one hundred reference styles for Biosciences journals, a similar number for those journals devoted to Medicine and a further twenty-five styles for Immunology journals. This compares with just one style for Mathematics journals! So, when presenting academic work, it is *essential* that the appropriate instructions be consulted before starting to write a manuscript. Expect problems from assessors, reviewers or editors if you do not conform to the house style for references.

### 5.4.3  A (fictitious) reference list

To illustrate the use of references in text and a reference list, you will find below a fictitious reference list including examples, some real (Sambrook *et al.*, 2001), others not (Brewer *et al.*, 1927, Dracula, 1897a), of different information sources, based on the Instructions for Authors for "*Microbiology*". This is an arbitrary choice used simply for illustrative purposes, and, of course, you would NEVER use fictitious references to support your coursework.

**Brewer, B., Stewer, J., Gurney, P., Davey, P., Whiddon, D., Hawke, H.** *et al.* **(1927).** On the road from Widdecombe Fair. *J Geogr* **12,** 1–10.

**Dracula, C. (1897a).** Blood disorders; a source for concern? *Vox Sang* **34,** 4–8.

**Dracula, C. (1897b).** Blood-borne infection; a source for concern? *Haematol Bluttrans* **56,** 123–140.

**Dracula, C. (1898).** A review of blood disorders in the Transylvanian populace. *Haemophilia* **78,** 5–14.

**Frankenstein D. R., Igor, N. M. & Other, A. N. (1818).** On the regeneration of human tissues. *Nature Biotechnol* 9, 333–345.

**Jekyll, D. R. (1888).** Lycanthropes wolf their food: a prospective study. *Vet Surgery* **10,** 666-668.

**Jekyll, D. R. & Hyde, M. R. (1886).** The unfortunate case of Mr H. In *Ghoulies and Ghosties and Long-leggety Beasties and Things that Go Bump in the Night*, pp 1–25. Edited by A. Spectre. Cluj-Napoca: Nosferatu Press.

**Leeds University Library (2007)** References and citations explained. [online]. University of Leeds. Available from: http://library.leeds.ac.uk/info/200201/training/218/references_and_citations_explained [Last accessed 11th September 2008].

**Sambrook, J., Fritsch, E. & Maniatis, T. (2001).** *Molecular Cloning: a Laboratory Manual*, 3rd edn. Cold Spring Harbor, NY: Cold Spring Harbor Laboratory Press.

**van Helsing, A. (1893).** *A study of the blood disorders of the population of Transylvania.* PhD, University of Guttenberg.

The first reference is to a multi-author paper that could have appeared in *Journal of Geography*. Old Uncle Tom Cobley was the team leader but he was the seventh author on the paper and does not appear in the citation, other than as "*et al.*". Next, there is a reference to one of two papers published by Dr Dracula as sole author in 1897. This may have appeared in the journal "*Vox Sanguinis*". It is followed by a reference to Dracula's second paper of that year, which may have been found in "*Haematologie und Bluttransfusion*". Following this reference is a single paper by Dracula again, appearing in 1898, possibly in the journal "*Haemophilia*". The paper by the Frankenstein team that could have appeared in 1818 may be found in *Nature Biotechnology*. Dr Jekyll is one of two authors of a paper that may be seen in *Veterinary Surgery*. He also wrote a chapter in a book edited by Prof. Spectre and published by the Nosferatu Press, which is located in Cluj-Napoca, the capital of Transylvania. Sambrook *et al.* wrote the *Molecular Cloning* book, published by Cold Spring Harbor Laboratory Press, located in New York. This is a real reference, as is the online citation to the University of Leeds web page on citing references. Lastly, you are shown a fictitious PhD thesis from a university that does not exist and written by one Abraham van Helsing.

### 5.4.4 *Compiling a reference list*

References in your reference list should refer to the actual source material that you consulted, **not** to the URL of the database in which you found your reference.

References in the list should be ordered as follows:

- alphabetically by surname of the first authors
- then, for any given first author, single-authored papers come before jointly authored papers
- within these categories (single-authored by X, then jointly authored with X as first author), the order is chronological

For the journal *Microbiology*, references should be formatted as follows:

1. surnames (in bold font) come first; include a comma after the surname followed by the initials (in bold) of that author. Each initial should be followed by a full stop and a space, and
   i. with up to six authors in a reference, separate author names by a comma immediately after the full stop of the last initial and separate the last two author names by an ampersand, "&"
   ii. generally, if there are more than six authors contributing to a paper, all those appearing after the sixth author are listed as "*et al.*", although sometimes you may be required to cite every author

2. year of publication (bracketed and in bold) followed by a full stop
3. title of the article in regular font, but using italics where appropriate for Latin names, etc.
4. title of the source of the citation, with titles of journals abbreviated according to the Institute for Scientific Information

Additional information and different formats may be required when referencing specific types of source (journal, book, thesis or internet) as shown in the following sections.

Difficulties with listing all the authors arise for papers to which a very large number of authors have contributed, such as the following, with 976 authors (imagine entering all those into a reference list!):

> **Van de Werf, F., Adgey, J., Ardissino, D., Armstrong, P. W., Aylward, P., Barbash, G., *et al.* (1999).** *Single-bolus tenecteplase compared with front-loaded alteplase in acute myocardial infarction: the ASSENT-2 double-blind randomised trial. Lancet,* **354**, 716–722.

## References to journal articles

Abbreviated journal titles are given in italics **without full stops**; one-word titles are given in full. This is followed by the volume number of the journal (in bold), and then immediately by a comma. The citation is completed by citing the first and last pages of the paper, separated by a hyphen.

## References to books

Following on from the title, these should also include the edition, editor(s) (if any), town of publication and publisher, in that order. When the reference is to a particular part of a book, the inclusive page numbers and the chapter title must be given.

## References to a thesis

This is sometimes necessary. The citation should appear as follows: family name of the author, initial(s), (year), title, type of qualification, academic institution granting the degree.

## References to electronic resources

As yet, there is no standard method, so the recommendations below are intended as guidance for those needing to cite such sources of information now. Documents on internet sources can be identified by the URL (uniform resource locator) or internet address. **Note:** with long URLs be careful to split only after the forward slashes in the address, and do not add further punctuation, such as hyphens, or alter the case of any characters in the address.

Give as much of the following information as is available: author/editor, year, title [online], (edition), place of publication, publisher (if ascertainable), available from: URL [date of last access].

If no author is specified, you should ascribe authorship to the smallest identifiable organizational unit (the standard method for citing works produced by a corporate body).

If the date of publication is not available, write "No date". It may be possible, in some cases, to find the date on which the page was created when using *Internet Explorer*, by right-clicking on a page and choosing "Properties" from the menu.

The term "online" in square brackets indicates the "type of medium" and is used for all internet sources. These may include, for example, ftp or Gopher sites, as well as web pages. The term publisher is used here to cover both the traditional idea of a publisher of printed sources, as well as organizations responsible for maintaining sites on the internet. The "date of last access" is the date on which you viewed or downloaded the document. This allows for any subsequent modifications to the document common with this medium of communication.

Occasionally you may need to cite other sources of information. You should seek advice from your tutors or library team on such citations.

### 5.4.5 *Citing references in your text*

When citing a paper by **a single author**, your reference should consist of the author's surname, followed by a comma and then the date that the paper was published: for example (Dracula, 1897). If a paper has **two authors**, use "&" to join the authors rather than "and". Thus, you should write (Jekyll & Hyde, 1886) **not** (Jekyll and Hyde, 1886). For papers with **more than two authors**, use "*et al.*", as in (Frankenstein *et al.*, 1818). Note that "*et al.*" ends with a full stop, to denote that it is an abbreviation.

References to **different papers by the same author(s) in the same year** should be distinguished in the text and the reference list by the letters a, b, etc. Suppose Dracula was prolific in 1897. His works may be cited in the text of a report as (Dracula, 1897a) and (Dracula, 1897b) or, if citing two references together (Dracula, 1897a, b). If you need to cite a **group of references together**, it is recommended that you cite the earliest reference first. If you have **more than one citation for a given year**, then references should be cited in alphabetical order for that year. Each reference in a group should be separated with a semi-colon. If all the references used in the examples above were to be cited together, the result would look like this: (Frankenstein *et al.*, 1818; Jekyll & Hyde, 1886; Dracula, 1897a, b).

## 5.5 How to write a good essay

### 5.5.1 *General considerations*

Imagine that you are marking essays. If you were confronted with a large pile of scripts to mark what would **you** welcome most, and what would you hate?

A well-structured essay that shows clarity of thought and is legible is a joy to mark. Essays that are full of waffle, and that do not address their subjects are a real turn-off. How can you make sure your work is in the welcome category rather than being the most hated?

Any well-written essay or report requires information to be delivered in a well-defined structure with a beginning, a middle and an end (see Table 5.1): poor essays from inexperienced students often lack the beginning and end sections.

**Table 5.1 Anatomy of an essay**

| | |
|---|---|
| The beginning or "the introduction"; – this places the subject of the essay in its context | Here, you define the subject of the essay. You do this so your reader knows whether to read on or not. <br><br> Try to engage your reader with your topic to "persuade" him or her to continue, particularly if you are hoping to have your essay marked. <br><br> Consider for whom the essay is being written. Do they have sufficient specialist knowledge to allow you to assume that they already have considerable insights into the topic? Or is your readership drawn from a broad background where you will need to include sufficient background material to allow them to follow your arguments? <br><br> This is where you need to define the terms of your essay and explain your strategy. For example, you may give a brief overview of a broad topic in the introduction, reserving the in-depth exploration of selected examples to the body of your essay. |
| The middle or "the body"; – this is where you address the subject of your essay and develop ideas | This contains a series of linked arguments, each of which may have an introduction, a body and a summary. Depending on the length of the essay, you may consider splitting the body into different sections: <br><br>     Point 1 <br>         Theme 1.1 <br>         Theme 1.2 <br>     Point 2 <br>         Theme 2.1 <br>     etc… <br><br> Even if you don't make formal subdivisions in your essay, it is likely that you will break the body of your work naturally. At the simplest level, you will divide your text into paragraphs, each of which should be a self-contained unit expressing one idea. <br><br> If the essay title was in the form of a question, **make sure that you answer it in this section of the essay.** |
| The end or "conclusion"; – this is where you should summarize the topic | This is where you make explicit the points you consider to be of most importance. Never introduce into your conclusions new material or ideas that are not covered previously in the essay. <br><br> This is also a place where you should highlight any areas of uncertainty regarding the topic. You may wish to make suggestions as to how, in future, these uncertainties may be resolved. |

### 5.5.2 *What is found in a good essay*

In broad terms, this classification can be related to Honours Degrees. Below, you will find a rough guide to what university tutors look for in answers of different classes.

### *First class answers*

Students who gain first class marks take an "extended abstract" approach to writing essays. Here, topics in the essay are not only related to one another in a cohesive structure but, when relevant, they are related to wider body of knowledge and show an understanding of "the question behind the question". Students who attain first class marks link related topics and analyse information in depth.

### *Upper second class answers*

Upper second class marks are the reward of those who apply a "relational" method to their writing. In this case, relevant topics are related to one another in an overall structure and are linked to form a cohesive argument, rather than being simply listed in text.

### *Lower second class answers*

People who do not often progress beyond a basic approach to the set topic generally obtain lower second class marks. Here, ideas are considered independently in the essay, rather than being linked with one another.

### *Third class answers*

Third class essays are written by students who just do not engage properly with the topic. Their work tends to be superficial, poorly organized, inaccurate and missing essential details, in addition to showing an absence of appropriate links between topics. There may be major errors and/or omissions from the text and irrelevant material is often present. Poorly worded and ungrammatical essays will also attain lower class marks.

### *Poor answers*

These arise for two basic reasons.

1. Sometimes the writer does not understand the topic, or what the title is asking for, and so finds it impossible to put the right information together in a logical order.
2. Other times, the student simply hasn't spent enough time researching the topic and thinking about what information is required to address the title appropriately, or how to put the information together in a logical way. Starting your essay the night before it is due to be handed in is often the cause of the problem!

### 5.5.3 *Assessing essays*

How would you assess these short essays? If you were asked to mark them, to which of the three versions of a short essay devoted to cholesterol would you give the highest marks?

## Version 1

*A major ampipathic polar lipid, cholesterol, possesses both hydrophobic and hydrophilic regions. Cholesterol is an essential steroid lipid substance present in varying degrees in virtually every animal membranes constituting approximately 25% of the membrane lipids in certain nerve cells of all animal membranes. The great importance of cholesterols presence is it's capability of transportation of fatty acids, the metabolism of fatty acids and the production of hormones such as oestrogen and progesterone formation of vitamin D for the skin and formation of bile acids for food digestion. Nevertheless, for the insulation of nerve fibre's from damage. Conversely, excess cholesterol can cause diseases and death by depositing in certain areas of the arteries causing blockage leading to health problems such as heart diseases.*

*For the above advantages and disadvantages of cholesterol, cholesterol exists in the blood as two types, high density lipoproteins and low density lipoprotein. Both these lipoproteins differ in their densities upon which transport is based. Their combinations of lipids and proteins present vary depending on the particular lipoprotein, though they do similarize in their structure of a hydrophobic shell of proteins and a hydrophobic lipid core and amphipathic lipids. It is according to their lipid content that their role is determined, for example, HDL consists merely of a greater proportion of protein than lipids, therefore rich in phospholipids and cholesterol.*

## Version 2

*To the public, cholesterol is probably the most famous and well-known lipid. It had long been accused by health professionals as the prominent cause of human cardiovascular diseases. Non-health professionals all think of it as a bad thing. But is it? To many health conscious people who didn't bother to check their facts, it may come as a shock to know that cholesterol has a crucial role in the structures of cell membranes and is a precursor of steroid hormones, bile acids and even vitamin D. The "good side" of cholesterol has not been well advertised at all. Therefore we should take time to explore this important lipid – is it really the culprit guilty of causing the death of millions of people worldwide?*

*To produce a balanced discussion, we will look first at what the body does with its cholesterol to see where things might go wrong. Cholesterol is not soluble in water, so the body uses "packages" of special types of proteins and fats called lipoproteins, to carry it around the blood. There are many different types, such as low-density lipoproteins (LDL), high-density lipoproteins (HDL), very low-density lipoproteins (VLDL) etc. which carry different amounts of cholesterol. LDLs carry the highest proportion of cholesterol and are considered "bad" by doctors since they are associated with heart disease and stroke. On the other hand, HDLs have a low proportion of cholesterol and are the "good guys" of the lipoprotein world.*

## Version 3

*Cholesterol is an essential component of virtually every animal membrane, and comprises up to 25% of lipid in some nerve membranes. It is also important in the transportation and metabolism of fatty acids, in the production of hormones such as oestrogen, progesterone, in the formation of Vitamin D in the skin and in the formation of bile acids, which aid the digestion of food. Although cholesterol is essential, excess quantities can lead to health problems such as heart disease and in severe cases, death. The reasons why cholesterol, which is such an essential component of eukaryotic cells, can become a 'killer' will be explored in the following essay.*

*Cholesterol is carried in the blood as a constituent of high- and low-density lipoproteins (HDLs and LDLs respectively). The lipoproteins differ in their composition (which determines their densities) and they have a common structure of a hydrophobic lipid core and a hydrophilic shell. The higher density of the HDLs compared to LDLs is due to a greater proportion of proteins, phospholipids and cholesterol.*

Did you note that Version 1 is full of grammatical errors? The second sentence talks of "every animal membranes", where "every animal membrane" is what is required. The next sentence has "it's" where the meaning is the possessive "its". "Nevertheless, for the insulation of nerve fibre's from damage" doesn't contain a verb and so is not a sentence. And things go downhill from there.

You may have found that the tabloid newspaper style and repeated questions fired at the reader in Version 2 is better but they make this a challenging read. Version 3, which avoids flashy style tricks and, consequently, appears authoritative is more likely to score best.

---

**Checklist for writing good essays**

- A good essay has a beginning, a middle, and an end.
- Figures and/or tables are welcome in essays but they need to be numbered unambiguously in the body of the text.
- When figures and/or tables are included, they should have a title; ideally they should also have a short explanatory legend.
- Scientific writing should be in the "third person".
- Try to achieve clarity of style; do not use long words and complex sentences designed to impress as very often they have the opposite effect.
- Avoid waffle in your essay.
- Stick to the subject set, rather than the topic you want to write about that sounds like it may be close.
- Read your work out loud and re-write the text until it "flows".
- *AVOID PLAGIARISM* – passing off someone else's work as your own is dishonest and carries severe penalties, culminating in exclusion from university.

---

### 5.5.4 *Planning your essay*

This is a very personal activity, and you may well find the following suggestions are not appropriate for you. We do, however, offer the following steps as one model for writing successful essays.

> **Steps in planning your essay**
>
> Step 1
> - Obtain the title.
> - Gather your thoughts on the topic and make notes.
> - Prepare a rough outline of your ideas.
> - Perform your literature search.
>
> Step 2
> - Prepare the first draft of your essay.
>
> Step 3
> - PAUSE and re-read the first draft.
>
> Step 4
> - Now write your second draft.
> - PAUSE AGAIN and consider asking a friend for constructive criticism.
>
> Step 5
> - You are now ready to write your essay.

This should show you why it always takes longer to write an essay than you think it will. Let's explore the steps in more detail.

## Step 1

Consider the title carefully and then jot down a few notes on the areas that you want to cover.

> *"Discuss the statement that the three-hour written examination paper is something that most graduates will not face again and fails to test skills necessary for a professional scientist. How best should these skills be assessed to permit determination of the degree class of a science graduate if not through traditional examinations?"*

If you were faced with this question, you should jot down your initial ideas. The question assumes that all graduates will pursue a career in science – is this valid? Practical training is under threat, and it may be argued that students are already doing too little at the cutting edge to allow for a meaningful assessment of these skills that could contribute to degree classification. This guide has already identified the areas that are considered important for graduates: personal skills, problem-solving and critical analysis, retrieval and handling of information, communication skills, teamwork.

Your essay may address some or all of these topics. Before long, you will have a number of headings that will form the body of your essay.

You can generate your notes in different ways.

- You could jot down what you know about a topic and then think about what information you consider to be the most important. From this, you could draw up a list of ideas, ranked in order of importance. These rankings then form the subheadings of the essay.

- Alternatively, you could produce a "mind map", a "spider diagram" or "spray", which are excellent ways of brainstorming a topic. To produce your mind map, start with the BIG IDEA in the centre of a blank piece of paper. Think of the topics that relate to the BIG IDEA and arrange these around the central figure. Some of these may lead to subtopics and to even more ideas. If you link your ideas with lines, you quickly build up a picture that looks like a web – hence the use of the term "spider diagrams" (see Figure 5.1). You do not need to restrict yourself to words – pictures can be incorporated into your diagram.

**Figure 5.1 How ideas link in an essay**

There is software available to help you to generate your mind map which allows you to play around with the arrangement of ideas very easily. In Figure 5.2, the subtopics have become sections of the essay and the rearrangement of the different branches makes it look much more like an essay layout. It is important that *you have a good idea of the outline of the essay before you start an in-depth literature search*. If you do not do this, then you may waste considerable time reading irrelevant material.

The internet is a frequently used source of initial information but it **must be used with great care** as explained earlier in this chapter. Having read your initial reference material, you may discover that you have not yet covered everything necessary for your essay, or you may decide that you have given greater prominence to particular ideas than they really need. At this stage, it is a relatively simple task to adjust the balance of your essay plan.

## Step 2

**Draft the essay.** Find a quiet hour or so to write out a draft of the essay, at one sitting if possible, without too much detail at this stage. This will illustrate what you will need in your final introduction, body and summary. When writing this draft, you should bear in mind the suggestions on style and the use of good English, as set out previously.

## Step 3

**Re-read the draft,** perhaps after leaving it aside for a day or two. Is it logical and are the ideas inter-related? Have you kept to the topic? Have you said what you want to say? If the answers are yes, yes and yes then you are ready to go on to the next stage.

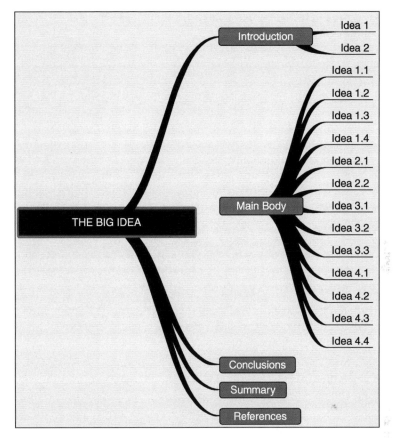

**Figure 5.2 How linked ideas in an essay may become ordered**

## Step 4

**Prepare a second, fuller draft** – if there is time, put this second draft aside for a week or so, before the final stage.

## Step 5

**Prepare the final paper** – if you are feeling brave, then you might like to ask a friend for constructive criticism. This is a useful exercise to ensure that you are really saying what you think you are saying. Check the spelling and grammar, and when you are finally satisfied with your effort, then you are ready to submit your essay.

## Step 6

**Submit the essay.** You should only hand in an essay when you are convinced that it is the best that you can achieve in the time available to you. It is essential not to delete the working file of your essay, or any other work, until after the work has been marked and returned, and the module has concluded after the marks have been published. We are all human, and markers do lose work occasionally.

## 5.6 How to write a practical report

At some point, you will be required to write a report of your practical work. The style of report that is required is an amalgam of those used for the principal journals devoted to the publication of scientific research and it is essential that you follow this style. Your report is intended to communicate your results and conclusions, so it is very important to pay attention to the use of good English. It should also be presented clearly, neatly and with precision. You may need to present your reports using a word processor. Although this will give you a basic level of neatness, paying attention to the layout will bring dividends. Often you will be required to show the results of mathematical calculations. Except for the simplest of calculations, it is essential to show your workings. Unless you do, you will inevitably be penalized if you make a mistake. If you show your workings it is easier for the person who is marking your work to see where you went wrong and to provide you with appropriate feedback so that you will avoid the problem in future. Get into the habit of making "guesstimates" of the result that you may expect. Checking your graphs and results against your "guesstimate" will show if the results you wish to present are sensible.

Your report should be written in the third person, past tense. It should comprise a title page, introduction, methods, results, discussion, and references.

---

**Common problems that you should avoid in practical reports**

- A lack of organization such that information is not presented in a logical order.
- Disjointedness: each section should lead naturally into the next section.
- A lack of focus such that there is too much irrelevant information or not enough relevant information.
- A lack of critical rigour.
- Accepting all published papers at face value; just because something is published in peer-reviewed literature it need not necessarily be correct. There may be other papers presenting opposing views with equally convincing arguments, so you should always retain a critical view of what you read.
- Poor use of references; use of too many references that are too old to be of value; references that are not cited accurately; excessive reliance on reviews; references that are biased towards one research group; citing too few papers to support the arguments being expounded.
- Being too long!

---

### 5.6.1 The title page

This should begin with the title of your investigation, which should be appropriate to the work in the report and descriptive of the experiment that you have carried out. You must also include a unique identifier such as your name or student ID number, so that the mark may be attributed to you and the work returned after marking.

### 5.6.2 The introduction

This should include a description of the background information that relates to your experiment(s), written in your own words and including material beyond that provided in the practical schedule, when relevant. You should conclude the introduction by stating the aims of the experiment.

| Checklist for a good introduction |
| --- |
| • Give essential background information. |
| • Set the scene. |
| • Put forward the aims of the study. |
| • Be succinct. |

### 5.6.3 The methods section

When included, this should contain a concise description of the methods that you used, with sufficient detail to allow an experienced scientist to repeat your experiment without having to consult other sources. You will not always be required to include a methods section. For some exercises, this section is omitted entirely: on other occasions, you will only need to describe changes to the method provided for that particular exercise. Remember, however, that it is your responsibility to check what is required for each report. As with the introduction, this section should be written in your own words rather than being copied from the practical schedule that you were given to carry out the experiment. Try to avoid using too many linking phrases, such as *"and then we did this... and then we did that"* or *"...following this..."* or *"...following that..."*. Another common phrase in poor reports is *"...and then this was done..."*. A better way of phrasing material may be: *"Recordings were made after the light intensity in the bat cave had been adjusted"*. The methods section should be written as descriptive text rather than as a list or recipe.

### 5.6.4 The results section

This must be a text-based description of your observations that will include appropriate figures and/or tables. Your investigation may produce large quantities of "raw" data that will need to be refined before presentation in a practical report, and you will need to perform simple calculations to derive a useful set of data. For example, you may need to convert absorbance readings from an enzyme experiment into molar rate of change in concentration. Sometimes, when you first encounter a set of calculations it can appear that what is required of you is complicated and confusing. The more you practise, however, the easier calculations will become. It is a good idea to review all of the information that you have to carry out the required calculation.

**Do not** start your results section with a table or figure. In the early part of your undergraduate studies, you may be asked to provide data in the form of both figures and tables to check that you can draw accurate figures from your data; however, unless you are asked specifically for them, you should not present data twice. This convention is used for scientific papers and is good practice in scientific communication.

Unless you are describing complex pieces of work, where the results from one experiment lead on to the design of further investigations, you should not draw any conclusions in the results section of your report.

## Presentation of results in a table

Raw data are often refined before they are presented in tables. When you use more than one table or figure, you should name them using sequential numbers (Table 1, Table 2, Table 3, etc.) and refer to them each in the text so that your readers can locate the correct figure or table with ease. Tables should include a short legend and should be presented neatly and, depending on the data that you are presenting, without gridlines. In Figure 5.3, which is easier to interpret: Table X or Table Y?

Table X. Presentation of results within a grid

| Classification | Result |
|---|---|
| 1 | X units |
| 2 | Y units |
| 3 | Z units |

Table Y. Presentation of results without using a grid

| Classification | Result |
|---|---|
| 1 | X units |
| 2 | Y units |
| 3 | Z units |

**Figure 5.3  Presentation of data in a table with or without gridlines**

With complex data and large tables, gridlines may guide the reader through the mass of information. With simple tables, however, reducing the lines in a grid makes the data more accessible. To see the effect of gridlines, look through papers published in the peer-reviewed scientific literature and see if you can find any presented in a full grid.

When appropriate, you should present the results of any statistical work that you have carried out to analyse your results. This should be descriptive and embedded in the body of the text. Do not be tempted just to cut and paste the results from your favourite statistics software package. If nothing else, by describing your results you will gain insight into what they mean.

## Effective use of results

Having obtained your set of data, it is important that the best use should be made of the results. There are many types of figure from which you should choose the most appropriate format for the best presentation of your data: histograms, line graphs, scatter plots, pie charts, box plots, micrographs, diagrams, traces from instruments, etc. The most useful charts are likely to be line, bar or column graphs and scatter charts. However, pie charts can be effective, for example, in the presentation of the composition of fluids or populations of species in different habitats. **Be aware that for some reports, computer-generated plots are not always appropriate and hand-drawn plots are the preferred method of presentation of data.** *Appendix C, Section 5* gives advice on how to present your data using *Microsoft Excel* and *Catch Up Maths & Stats* gives more detailed advice on how to analyse and present data.

---

**A note about units**

Remember that all observations must be expressed together with their proper units. In a calculation this is a very useful way of ensuring that you have performed the calculation correctly because, if you are unsure which terms would be divided or multiplied by each other, the units can often be a guide. Units should combine or cancel out to give final terms that are appropriate to the required answer regardless of the numerical calculations involved. By forgetting to include appropriate units in a calculation, you may make errors and have no easy way of checking at which step you have gone wrong.

---

All figures should be numbered and include a legend in which the salient features are described succinctly. When appropriate, you should provide a key to the elements of the figure. The key may be included in the legend or may be part of the figure itself.

## Independent and dependent variables

If a graph is the most appropriate form to represent your data, the "independent" variable should be plotted on the x-axis (horizontal or *abscissa*); with the "dependent" variable on the y-axis (vertical or *ordinate*). It is important to show all data points on graphs and it may be necessary to include error bars to indicate the spread of your results. The axes of your graph must be labelled to include the units in which your observations were measured.

## Which is more useful, a curve or a straight line?

The two graphs below (Figure 5.4 and Figure 5.5) show the same data represented in different ways. Both show that the population grows with increasing rapidity as time progresses. Trying to read the population size accurately at the later times in the first graph becomes difficult due to the increasing slope. Therefore, the most useful graph is one in which the data points lie on a straight line, i.e. Figure 5.5. The data here have been "transformed" into a straight line by plotting the logarithm of the population size against time:

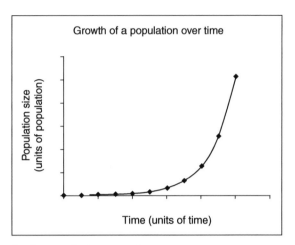

**Figure 5.4 Growth of a population over time.**
These data have been plotted without transformation.

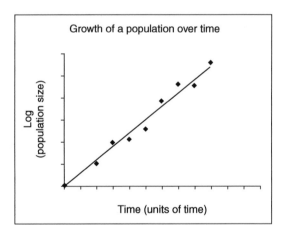

**Figure 5.5 Growth of a population over time.**
These data have been plotted after converting numbers of individuals in a
population to the logarithm of the number of individuals.

## The best fit line

Any experimental observation is prone to error and so it is very unlikely that all of your
data points will lie on a straight line for any experiment that you ever perform. Your
points are much more likely to be scattered on either side of the "line of best fit".

The "best" straight line may not pass through any of the data points. Drawing the
"best" straight line on any graph takes practice and experience. As a rough guide,
however, the "best" line will have as many points above the line as fall below it
(assuming you have an even number of observations, of course). In Figure 5.4, the line
passes through the origin of the graph. but do not assume that all results will conform

to this. You should decide if it is appropriate for your line of best fit to pass through the origin or not. Also, remember that lines of best fit are not necessarily straight lines!

## Handling data using Microsoft Excel

In some instances you may be able to use computer software to help with data handling. *Microsoft Excel* can be invaluable for handling repetitive calculations, for organizing data, and for presenting data as charts and graphs; it can also carry out some statistical analysis. Data are arranged in a spreadsheet with each cell (i.e. box in the grid) containing a single numerical value, or some text or a formula. Calculations can be performed on whole rows or columns of numbers simultaneously, saving many hours of laborious work. A big bonus is that if the value of any of the numbers in the spreadsheet changes, all the calculations involving that number will automatically be altered. By using *Excel* efficiently you can save a great deal of time and are likely to make fewer numerical errors when handling calculations involving large sets of data. Moreover, *Excel* allows you to express your data in a variety of chart formats, as explained in *Appendix C*.

If you produce and format tables in *Microsoft Excel* you can then transfer them straight into *Microsoft Word*. Additionally, it is possible to move data from a *Word* document into *Excel* for further processing.

## Trendlines

The line of best fit can be calculated using "regression analysis", a very useful statistical tool which can also fit non-linear functions. To illustrate this, Figure 5.6 shows the line of best fit for a drug bioassay. In this experiment, samples containing antibiotic were placed in wells in an agar plate that was pre-seeded with a susceptible test organism. The more antibiotic present in a sample, the bigger was the zone of inhibition around the well containing the sample. In this graph, the

**Figure 5.6 Line of best fit from a drug assay.**
This figure is a screen shot from a *Microsoft Excel* spreadsheet used to find the trendline from this assay.

trendline does not pass through the origin but through the *y*-axis at the value of the diameter of the wells in which the samples were placed. The individual datum points were quite scattered and it can be seen that the trendline is curved. *Microsoft Excel* also calculated the equation of the line of best fit.

It is important that whenever you use standard curves to determine the value of an unknown sample, **any value for your "unknown" is interpolated from within the range of data points that you have obtained.** You should not be tempted to extrapolate your data beyond the lowest and highest values observed. There is no guarantee that the beautiful continuous curvilinear relationship seen in your data will, or should, extend beyond the limits of your observations.

**Finally,** you should always remember that there will be errors in your readings and you must take them into account when assessing any results you may obtain.

---

**Checklist for a good results section**

- Prepare figures and tables, if required, *before* writing the text.
- Plan the layout of the section.
- Present the results in a logical order, not necessarily in the order that the work was performed.
- Use section headings, if appropriate.
- Introduce each section, explaining why the work was considered important to the development of your ideas.
- Unless *specifically* told otherwise, use a figure *or* a table, but *not both.*
- Figures and tables must be self-contained and as such do not need to be confined to the results section – they may be used anywhere to enhance the clarity of the idea or to summarize complex information.
- When using figures you should:
  - ask yourself what you really need to show
  - show each individual data point on line graphs
  - plot the "independent" variable – what you choose to observe – on the *x*-axis
  - show error bars when appropriate, even on histograms
  - avoid crowding too many separate graphs into one figure
  - label axes and choose scales carefully
  - remember to provide a key for each figure
- Only use illustrations if they are of good quality.
- Remember that illustrations may need special preparation.
- Be aware that there is no such thing as a "typical" gel or micrograph – these can take weeks of preparation!
- Remove surplus material from images but be careful to retain all useful information.
- Label illustrations carefully and clearly.

---

**Here is another reminder:** a numerical result requires the inclusion of appropriate units.

### 5.6.5 The discussion section

This is where you should discuss *all* of the results that you have presented in the previous section. Points that you may like to consider include:

- are the results accurate?
- are the results within the expected range of results for the experiment? If not, what might have gone wrong?
- do the results confirm or refute results from other experts? You should supply references to published information.

If the practical schedule from which you were working poses questions, the discussion section is the place where these should be addressed. You should highlight the significant findings of your experiment and discuss their importance. Your final paragraph should comprise the conclusions that you draw from your study.

You should finish your report with a reference list. References can be cited, both within the text and in the reference list, in a variety of ways and you should follow the guidelines given for your particular exercise carefully.

---

**Checklist for a good discussion section**

- Decide what constitutes your main findings.
- State clearly each of the main findings and discuss their relevance and implications.
- State how your findings compare with the work of others and cite references to relevant published papers.
- When necessary, refer back to previous sections of your report.
- Did you answer the question posed? If not then you will need to explain why not.
- What overall conclusions can you draw from your observations?
- What further work would you perform to follow up your observations or to support your argument?

---

**What to avoid in your discussion**

- Restating the results instead of interpreting them.
- Not putting your findings into a proper context.
- Repeating material presented in the introduction.
- Adopting a disorganized or illogical structure.
- Unclear and/or confused conclusions.

# 5.7 Posters

Posters are often used to communicate recent findings at conferences and other scientific meetings because they are one of the most efficient ways of presenting scientific research to a wider audience. Poster presentation sessions give authors the opportunity to discuss their work informally with other research workers and to pass on practical tips and techniques. Effective posters are those that explain the topic and the work undertaken clearly and are presented in a well-organized and logical manner. Guidelines for the style of presentation may differ according to the conference or course for which they are produced.

You should give careful thought to the presentation of your poster. A suggested format is shown in Figure 5.7. It will need a clear layout and should be readable at a distance. The basic structure requires an appropriate introduction, an outline of the work and a summary. Above all, it must make sense, giving reasons why you did the work and describing the conclusions that may be drawn from the results. The following points are worth bearing in mind.

- Remember that most people will probably spend only a few minutes reading your poster. You must get your message across in that time. Therefore, make sure your poster is succinct.

- Make use of short paragraphs or, preferably, bullet points rather than large blocks of text.

- Be ruthless in the material you discard. You do not have to report everything on your poster; you just need to tell a good story.

- Consider presenting your concepts and hypotheses as diagrams. Use figures or tables to summarize your results.

**Figure 5.7 Suggested plan for a poster**

Advice on preparing a poster using *Microsoft PowerPoint* can be found in *Appendix B, Section 8*.

To quote Jeremy Bentham:

> *"The more words there are, the more words there are about which doubts may be entertained".*

---

**Checklist to help you make good poster presentations**

- The poster should normally be produced in landscape format, unless you are told otherwise.
- Stick to the stated size limit.
- All text must be readable at a distance of 1 metre.
- Use at least 14 point text and preferably double space it.
- Photographs may be used and can be black and white or colour. If you do use photographs, make sure that you label them clearly.
- It is particularly important to remember to avoid large blocks of text on your poster.

---

# 5.8  Oral presentations

When first asked to make an oral presentation, many people feel apprehensive; this is perfectly normal. In this section, we give you advice that will help you to make effective oral presentations. Who knows, you may even end up enjoying them.

**The key to a good oral presentation is ensuring
that you are properly prepared.**

## 5.8.1  Planning

When planning your presentation it is important to bear in mind the following points.

- What level of knowledge of your audience can you assume? At university, most of the talks you will give will be to your fellow students and you will have a pretty good idea of the level of understanding they will have. Later in your career, however, you may well be required to give talks to much broader audiences and you will need to decide how to pitch your talk. This can be quite an art.
- What is the purpose of the presentation?
- How long is the presentation meant to last?
- Ensure that you have a clear vision of the information that you want to communicate.

## 5.8.2  Resources for delivery

Make sure you know what facilities will be available to you when you make your oral presentation. You will look pretty silly if you have spent days perfecting a

*PowerPoint* presentation only to find that the location in which you are speaking has no PC support, or that your beautiful acetate cannot be shown through lack of an overhead projector.

### 5.8.3 *Tips on using* **Microsoft PowerPoint**

These days, most presentations are made using *Microsoft PowerPoint*. While this is a very useful tool, it needs to be used with care. *PowerPoint* offers a bewildering array of backgrounds, most of which are horribly distracting; a minimalist approach often works best. Aim for a style and size of font that is simple and easy to read. Make sure that the colour of your text contrasts sufficiently with your background to enable the text to be read easily. Similarly, if you place images on a "busy" background, consider adding a border so that the image may be distinguished without difficulty. Cluttered diagrams and figures are a big turn-off for audiences.

*PowerPoint* has some wonderful gimmicks and animations. However, try not to use these over-enthusiastically. If every piece of text floats in and then pirouettes into its final resting place, your audience may well end up feeling mildly irritated or, worse, seasick. When it comes to animations, "*less is more*". Advice on using *Microsoft PowerPoint* may be found in *Appendix B*.

### 5.8.4 *Content and organization*

You are now ready to write your presentation. Like good essays, good oral presentations have three parts: a beginning, a middle, and an end (see Table 5.2).

**Table 5.2 Structure of a good oral presentation**

| Beginning or "Introduction" | This is where you grab the attention of your audience and inform them of the subject of the presentation. |
|---|---|
| Middle or "Main body" | This is where you need to present your information in a logical order. Good visual aids are extremely important to help explain systems and concepts. |
| End or "Conclusion" or "Summing Up" | Here, you should summarize the main points of your presentation, referring back to your introduction if possible. |

The advice on the structure of the presentation is the same as for a good lecture. To reiterate, you need to "…*tell them what you are going to tell them, you tell them, and then you tell them what you've just told them*"!

When designing your talk, it is worth remembering a few points.

- Assume that the information on an average *PowerPoint* slide will take about two minutes to deliver. So, assuming that you have an average amount of information, for a ten-minute talk, you should aim to have no more than six slides.
- Avoid information overload and so try not to have more than six lines of text per slide.

- Use short phrases rather than sentences so that the audience can focus on the main points.
- Avoid producing cluttered diagrams and figures.
- Check for spelling mistakes.

## 5.8.5 Practice

Having prepared your slides, your next task is to rehearse your talk. Try to get access to the room in which you will be making your presentation before the event so that you can get a feel for the ambience. Read your presentation aloud. This will highlight issues regarding timing and the sense of what you are trying to communicate. Although it may feel a little odd at first, rehearsing in conditions as close as possible to those for the real presentation will pay dividends.

> **Tip**
>
> Compile your "script" as a series of key points on index cards that act as aides-memoires. If you use more than one card for your script (one per key point?), it is a good idea to tie them together or number them in case you drop them during the talk itself.

### What to avoid for a good presentation

Do not be tempted to try to learn your presentation by heart. If you do, it is likely that your delivery will be rather stilted or you will forget your lines. Also, don't use a full script and read everything from that. For one thing, if you are using a text-based presenting tool like *PowerPoint*, your audience can read the key words faster than you can deliver them and, if your head is buried in your notes, your voice will not project to the back of the room. Worst of all, if you lose your place in the script, there will follow an embarrassed silence whilst you try to find where you had got to on the sheet! Finally, you will annoy your audience considerably if you decide simply to read your slides.

## 5.8.6 Your final presentation

Try to remember the following suggestions when you deliver your oral presentation.

### Face your audience and make eye contact as much as possible

But don't stare at any one individual. Do not be tempted to face the screen on which your talk is being projected since this alienates your listeners and your voice will not project out to the audience.

### Use a pointer

This helps to draw attention to specific parts of a slide or acetate. Be careful, however; large wooden canes do not make good props and they have been known to break if the speaker has rested on one too hard. Laser pointers bring their own hazards and should *never* be pointed at your audience. If your nerves get the better of you and you find the pointer wobbling about uncontrollably, why not use both hands to steady it? If you use acetates with an overhead projector, a pen can act as a pointer if it is laid on top of the acetate so the tip points to the relevant part.

## Pace your delivery

A good talk is not delivered at the same pace as you talk in normal conversation – it is somewhat slower. Interestingly, when you are nervous, the temptation is to speed up your delivery rather than slow it down. It is a good idea to introduce deliberate pauses into your delivery. This may seem strange at first, but it is a technique that works. If you watch videos of people making speeches, you can often count three beats between sentences – longer if the audience responds to the last point being made. Also, remember to take regular, large breaths. It does wonders for voice projection but it is something that can be easily overlooked if you are feeling nervous when presenting to a large group, many of whom you do not know. Regular breathing also forces pauses in your delivery, which is a good thing.

## Try to exude enthusiasm and confidence

This is commonplace amongst successful speakers. Don't panic if you find that you have accidentally skipped some information. If you are confident in your delivery, most of your audience won't notice, even if you have the relevant bullet point projected on screen. Confidence comes with knowing your topic. The better you know the subject about which you are talking, the more relaxed and comfortable you will be with your presentation. Remember, though, in almost any presentation that you will ever make, you will probably know more about the topic than most people in the audience.

### 5.8.7 Dealing with questions

After almost all oral presentations, your audience will have the opportunity to ask you questions. At first, this may seem daunting but you can prepare for this. While creating and constructing your presentation, think about the questions *you* would ask and make sure you have found the answers. If similar questions occur to your audience you are half way to answering them.

When you do get questions, answer the ones that have been asked, rather than trying to bend your answer to fit the question you would like to have been asked.

If you haven't heard the question properly, politely request the questioner to repeat it. If you don't know the answer, don't pretend that you do. You will only dig a hole for yourself and could end up looking seriously silly. If you do find that you are in a hole – stop digging!

Lastly, try to avoid foot-in-mouth disease. Think about what you are going to say before responding rather than spouting the first thing that comes into your head.

This was an experience of a postdoctoral student applying for a lecturing post, who avoided foot-in-mouth disease:

*"One of the interview panel was asking a long series of questions about the nature of mobile genetic elements when he suddenly asked me to name a third-generation cephalosporin. Given the series of questions that had gone before, I was somewhat taken aback. I paused rather than give a stupid answer. My interviewer barked back at me "Hurry up! They all begin with 'Cef-'". I continued my pause, and in my own time answered "ceftazidime" – the right answer; and I got the job."*

### 5.8.8 Improving your presentation technique

Once you have finished your presentation you can heave a huge sigh of relief. If, however, you want to make the most of the session, ask a trusted friend for constructive feedback. There are aspects of every presentation that can be improved. If you are ever asked to give advice, make sure criticism is constructive. Think about which you would prefer to hear: "That talk was rubbish" or "That talk went right over our heads. Next time why don't you try doing...". Also, the more times you give oral presentations, the easier they become.

---

**Checklist to help you make good oral presentations**

- Prepare thoroughly.
- Know your topic. The better you understand the topic you are presenting, the easier it will be to make an effective talk.
- Make sure you know what equipment, if any, will be available in the venue where you will talk.
- Don't overcrowd information onto visual aids and don't use backgrounds that are distracting.
- Make sure any text on your visual aids is readable.
- Use pictures, they are invaluable in good presentations.
- Use index cards containing a few key words only as an aide-memoire.
- Remember that you can fit in far less information per unit time than you think.
- Be confident in your presentation; look at the audience and speak clearly and relatively slowly.
- As soon as possible after the presentation, get constructive feedback from a friend (and be prepared to do the same for them).

---

# 5.9  Summative and formative assessment

In educational jargon, **"summative assessments"** are those that contribute to your final module mark. Many courses also make use of **"formative assessments"** which are assessments that provide guidance for you. They help you to know how you are getting on in the course, but they do not count towards your final module mark.

Formative assessment may be given in different ways. For example, it may come from tutors and laboratory demonstrators as written feedback on an assignment; helpful feedback will praise the good aspects of your work while pointing out any shortcomings to help you to see how you may improve in future assignments. Alternatively, electronic forms of feedback may be given if you use online learning packages. You will only understand what the feedback you receive means by looking carefully at the comments and at those aspects of your work to which they relate. You can then use this advice when producing future work. If you do not understand what the feedback means, it is important that you ask for clarification from the person who gave the feedback.

There is currently a move towards more self-directed learning. To ensure that your learning is appropriate, formative assessment will play an increasing role. Try to develop a systematic and productive approach to your feedback by using the checklist below; you might be surprised by how much your marks improve.

---

**Checklist for making the most of feedback**

- Keep a list of the most significant comments and what you understand these to mean.
- Recognize which aspects of your work are praised and make sure you keep doing these.
- Recognize which aspects of your work receive criticism and make sure you improve these in future work.
- Notice any recurring negative comments which might indicate that you do not understand how to correct problems that have been highlighted in previous work.
- Having done all this, you can then concentrate on the main aspects of your work that need improving while maintaining the things that you do well.

# Chapter 6  Using computers and information technology

At university, you will have plenty of opportunities to practise your computing skills and will have access to a range of software to help you with your studies. Immediately below, you will find general information; more specific advice on how to use the *Microsoft* software packages *Word*, *PowerPoint* and *Excel* more efficiently in your studies can be found in *Appendices A, B* and *C*, respectively.

**Word processors,** like *Microsoft Word*, are software packages for typing and arranging documents. You can easily cut and paste text, format your document, and mistakes are easy to rectify. Many word processors have spell-checking facilities and some can even check your grammar. Remember, however, they are all fallible and they may try to suggest changes to your writing that are patently stupid!

**Presentation – graphics software,** such as *Microsoft PowerPoint*, is used to make dynamic presentations that are valuable support material for your oral presentations.

**Spreadsheets,** including *Microsoft Excel*, are used for storing and sorting numerical data. They also perform calculations automatically. Many spreadsheets such as *Excel* can convert numerical data into a graphical presentation.

**Databases,** such as those produced using *Microsoft Access*, are collections of records somewhat like an old-fashioned card index. Because the computer does most of the hard work for you, databases can be linked together to provide very powerful information storage and retrieval – far more than could be imagined using a card-based system. Whereas spreadsheets, such as those produced using *Excel*, are viewed as a 'flat' or two-dimensional form, databases allow you to relate information between different spreadsheets simultaneously in a multi-dimensional manner. This is useful when you want to pick out and compare specific items of information about all the subjects in a group for which you have recorded a range of details. When setting up a database it is important to have decided *at the start* every one of the characteristics you wish to survey, otherwise you will have to trawl through each of the individual spreadsheets later, in order to add the extra details required. A detailed description of the *Microsoft* database, *Access*, is beyond the scope of this book and will not be included here.

**Statistical packages** are designed to take the hard work out of statistical calculations. You will be taught which statistical tests to use when in lectures and practical classes.

**Graphics packages** are commonly used by scientists to create graphs, pie charts, etc. They take the pain out of data presentation. These days such programs are often embedded in other packages such as spreadsheets.

# 6.1 Computer-based learning

Computer-based learning (CBL) packages are aids to learning that require the use of a computer. They may range from the simple multiple-choice question and answer program used to test your knowledge of a subject, through to simulations and computer models used to illustrate complex concepts that are difficult to present in any other way than through computer simulations. CBL is sometimes known as computer-assisted learning (CAL). Increasingly, CBL material is being delivered across the internet, meaning that you can access material from anywhere in the world. Another name for this is technology-enhanced learning, or TEL.

# 6.2 Being organized – file storage and management

It is important to get into the habit of being organized about storing your files with appropriate identifying names, and the files sorted into suitably ordered (and named) folders. Otherwise, you will very soon discover that keeping track of files becomes very hard, and that the document you really need to access, written just a couple of months previously, is lost in the morass of files that are in your folder. The Windows operating system allows you to do this, but beware the "default" save facility since this will keep adding files to the "My Documents" folder without placing the file into an appropriate folder. While you can choose any name for your folders, it is a good idea to give them logical names. Will you remember that you saved "mydoc1" or "coursework_4" in "the seventh circle of the seventh circle" weeks or months after you saved them? And will you remember what information each file contained? Figure 6.1 shows an example of a file structure that has a logical basis:

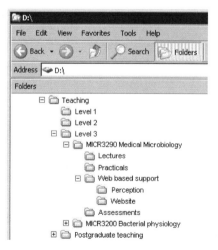

**Figure 6.1 An example of the file structure on a computer**

In this example you should note that the teaching folder contains separate folders for each level of study. In each will be sub-folders devoted to particular modules and these may contain sub-folders relating to teaching activities...

Jonathan Swift observed:

*"So, nat'ralists observe, a flea*
*Hath smaller fleas that on him prey,*
*And these have smaller fleas that bite 'em,*
*And so proceed ad infinitum".*

This has been expressed more poetically as:

*"Great fleas have little fleas upon their backs to bite 'em,*
*And little fleas have lesser fleas, and so ad infinitum.*
*And the great fleas themselves, in turn, have greater fleas to go on,*
*While these again have greater still, and greater still, and so on"*

So it is with file trees.

Organized file structures work best when you give your files logical names rather than relying on what your software assumes will be a sensible name – usually the first line of the text in the document.

# 6.3 Keep file sizes small

Although computer memory has probably never been so cheap and plentiful, you should occasionally pause to think about file sizes. Images cause a particular problem here. Using *Microsoft Paint*, the default file type is the "bitmap", where every dot in a picture has its position and colour recorded. This can generate enormous files, even for relatively small images. To overcome the problem of large file sizes for images, a number of other formats that compress your data have been developed. Among the most popular are "GIF" (short for *"Graphics Interchange Format"*) and the "JPG" or "JPEG" (derived from the name of the *"Joint Photographic Experts Group"*) file types. Both have advantages and disadvantages over each other (see Table 6.1). Another file format, the "PNG" or *"Portable Network Graphics"* file, overcomes many of the problems with GIF and JPG files, but it does not support animations.

# 6.4 Back-ups and passwords

With increasing numbers of students owing their own computers, migration of files between computers has become commonplace. Portable memory devices to use for such transfers have become much more reliable in recent years; nevertheless, they, and hard drives, do occasionally fail. This can be an extremely traumatic experience. If you are to avoid this, it is essential that you keep a back-up of files that are important to you on a CD-ROM, DVD, or a USB key.

**Table 6.1 Comparison of image file types**

|  | GIF | JPEG | PNG |
|---|---|---|---|
| Advantages | Good for saving line diagrams; can deliver animations | Good for complex images like photographs | Has file sizes intermediate between GIFs and JPEGs but with better colour depth |
| Disadvantages | Uses only 256 colours and so a high-resolution image may suffer from alterations in hue and some loss of definition | Suffers loss of definition around boundaries so text and clean lines may become blurred; the JPG format is not recommended for storing images that require subsequent editing since there is sequential loss of definition | Cannot display animations and not supported universally so some software packages cannot use this format |

It is also not unknown for computers to hang (just as you have finished your finest piece of work, but before you have saved it) losing your work and hours of your time. To avoid this problem, make sure you save your document every 5–10 minutes. On your own computer you can set it to save documents automatically at defined intervals, as explained in *Appendix A, Section 2.8*.

Many systems require a password before you can access the information you require. It is best not to use the same password for all these systems (access to an online bank account, academic resources and also your computer, for example), but if you have too many different ones you are liable to forget which ones apply to specific situations. To avoid this, you should keep a log of your passwords somewhere safe.

## 6.5 Email and etiquette

One of the advantages of email is that you can respond instantaneously to someone. Indeed, you can hold a "real-time" conversation. The speed with which you can communicate, however, can also be a disadvantage. Email communication is never subtle and it is all too easy to send an email that you may later regret sending. This is a particular problem when sending messages about which you have strong feelings. Remember that you can always save a draft of an email and send it later, having read it carefully before committing yourself to pressing the "send" button. Think about what effect your message may have on the recipient and ask yourself if you would want to receive the rant that you are about to send. What does it say about you? Likewise, beware of "humorous" email addresses. You can change your email alias easily, but do you really want to advertise to the world that you are a "studmuffin" or a "sexy_babe"? These are both names that students have used.

Remember, also, if you abuse university computing services, you will leave yourself open to disciplinary action being taken against you. In extreme cases, abuse has led to successful criminal prosecution.

## 6.5.1 Sending emails

Make sure you include a subject, so that the recipient knows what the mail is about when it arrives at the inbox. Some mailing programs will remind you to do this, but others don't.

You can send a message to more than one person by:

- including additional addresses in the 'To' box
- including addresses in the 'cc' box (carbon copy) – where addresses in the 'cc' box will appear on the recipients' email, or the 'bcc' box (blind carbon copy) which is useful if you don't want all the addresses to appear in the recipients' 'cc' box
- creating and using a distribution list containing email addresses of people you regularly want to contact (e.g. members of a committee) – this can save a lot of time

### Creating a message

Emails may be word processed in much the same way as documents in *Word*, including cutting and pasting, dragging and dropping, making bold and italic, etc. Clicking the right-hand button on the mouse can be used to activate sub-menus of useful operations and you can insert hyperlinks to web pages, so recipients are taken straight to the page by clicking on the link.

### Adding attachments

Use attachments to send large documents rather than trying to include them in the body of a standard mail message. Click on the attachments icon/box, and then browse for the file you require on the mini-file directory that appears. This facility is particularly useful for sending files such as coursework, CVs, minutes of meetings, pictures, and so on, to accompany a covering letter in the main email message.

> **Note**
>
> Try not to send large files (> 1 Mb) as attachments because they will not only slow the process of sending the mail but will also slow the recipient's receiver. Also, don't send attachments to large groups in a single email message. Very large attachments (such as detailed bitmaps or photographs) may require several minutes to download and can cause some computers to hang up. Always convert bitmap images to other, more compact formats before sending them as attachments to emails. In summary, try to keep emails small.

## 6.5.2 Etiquette

Although you may be informal amongst friends who know you well, remember that when you address others who know you less well (tutors, lecturers, prospective employers) they will form an opinion of you from what you write. Good sense says that you should make the effort to write in a grammatical and (reasonably) formal way that shows some respect to the recipient, otherwise you will appear off-hand, sloppy and rude. The box below summarizes the points to remember.

| What to do and not to do in emails | |
|---|---|
| Do:<br>• include a proper subject line to inform the recipient of the email contents<br>• begin with: *"Dear Dr / Prof. / Mr,"* etc.<br>• be polite and be grammatically correct, e.g. *"Thank you for contacting me about the meeting. I will be able to attend."*<br>• finish with your name (including surname). You might also want to include: *"Best wishes"* or *"Thank you"*, or *"I look forward to your reply"* | Do not:<br>• forget to include a subject<br>• begin with: *"Hi"*, *"Hiya"*, or even just launch into the main part of the message<br>• use slang, text language or sloppy grammar, e.g. *"yeh, il b ther 4 the mting"*.<br>• forget to include your name at the end (or the recipient might not be able to identify who has sent the message), or include: *"Luv Cherie x"*, or *"cya l8r"*, or *"thanx"* |

Email systems **usually** allow you to add a 'signature' to the end of your message – once set up this means that your title, position, address, phone number, etc. can be added automatically to each message you send.

## 6.5.3 Replying to messages

Be aware of the difference between the *'Reply to all'* and *'Reply'* buttons; the first will send your reply to all those in the 'cc' box AND the 'bcc' box, whereas the second will only reply to the sender. If your reply contains sensitive material, creating a new message to the sender alone might be the safer option. The message to which you reply will automatically appear in your reply but you can delete the non-essential parts of that message in order to save space.

## 6.5.4 Organizing your emails

Try to be tidy. Create folders within your mailer into which you can move related emails from your inbox (many systems allow you to do this simply by dragging and dropping). Delete unwanted emails so that your file space doesn't exceed any preset limit. If this happens, you may no longer be able to receive and send emails, which could have serious consequences if your department sends you information by email about important deadlines.

**DO NOT OPEN ATTACHMENTS** unless you are confident that they do not contain a virus. Always check:

- whether you know the sender – if you haven't any idea who they are, delete the file
- whether the subject looks sensible – ignore money-making offers, emails supposedly from banks or emails enticing you to augment parts of your anatomy! Even if these do not contain viruses, they are spam, they clog up the internet and should be deleted. Never reply to these because the organization will then 'retain' your email, send you more messages and sell your email address to other similar organizations.
- whether you were expecting an attachment – if you receive something odd, apparently from a friend, email them in a separate mail, to check that they really did send it
- the file format – those ending with .exe are executable files and may start a program running on your computer; they should be deleted immediately. Unfortunately file attachments with more common formats such as '.doc' may also contain viruses, so do check as per the first three points above before you open these files.

# 6.6 University printing services

An area where many students experience problems at some time during their degree is printing. You should remember that university printing facilities on campus are finite and demand for them is not spread evenly. So, if you rely on them, as the deadline for any assessment approaches, the length of printer queues grows with alarming rapidity and the time you have to wait to get your essay or report printed gets longer and longer. It is also all too easy to send multiple copies of a file for printing, particularly when you are under pressure. This will cost you money and it will create problems for other printer users. The last week of any term is a particularly bad time for printer queues, but any deadline for a large module can cause problems. Don't assume that because you don't have a deadline that there won't be a wait to get your words of wisdom into hard copy. There is a simple solution to this problem: *plan to get the work completed before the deadline.*

# 6.7 "To buy or not to buy; that is the question..."

Although you will be expected to use a variety of computer packages, you will not need to own a computer of your own. If they are required for a course, then access to the university's computers will be provided. Some people do prefer to buy their own computers, particularly for word processing. Some words of advice: a high-specification computer may cost you many hundreds of pounds, particularly if you buy the latest software packages, too; computer technology is progressing fast; second-hand machines have very little value, and once purchased, a new computer drops in value as fast as the price of holly in January. If you still want to buy a computer, decide what performance you really need for your personal work.

One final note of caution:

> *Computers can be used to achieve some wonderful work and they can be great fun. They can also become great time wasters. It is essential that you distinguish between computing for work and computing for pleasure!*

# Chapter 7  Revision and examinations

To misquote the late Bill Shankly on football, *"Examinations are not a matter of life or death. They are much more important than that"*.

Many students doubtless recognize this statement. The run-up to the exam period and exams themselves may feel like a nightmare, filled with panic, stress, anxiety attacks, caffeine fixes and wandering around like a zombie. You may also wake up in the middle of the night in a cold sweat, convinced that you haven't done enough revision. There are ways in which you can avoid the worst excesses of exam stress. You just need to decide that you will work hard and that you can succeed. Everything else will then follow from this.

**The keys to exam success are:**

- good organization
- self-discipline
- hard work

## 7.1  Effective revision

### 7.1.1  Plan a realistic revision schedule

This should be done well in advance of the examination date and you should think carefully about what you are trying to achieve. Only you know how much you have to cover and you will quickly discover how much you can achieve in a day so it is sensible to start in plenty of time. This means preparing a timetable so that you anticipate having completed your revision a few days before the date of your first examination. You should leave yourself time to spare so that you can cope with the unexpected. Furthermore, when you do end up with this unstructured time at the end of your revision, you can use it to go over those topics with which you are least happy. You should:

- remember that examinations test your knowledge and understanding over the **whole** subject area so you need to cover **all** of the topics covered in a module
- ask yourself if you want to cover something once, or several times; planning your time also means building in flexibility and breaks
- write out a realistic timetable covering all the topics that you need to revise

Detailed knowledge of a small part of the course will not compensate for large areas of ignorance. Students who do poorly in module exams based on essay-style questions, often do so because, although they can tackle two questions with ease, they have not revised enough of the module to permit them to tackle a third topic adequately. This is painful and is best avoided.

### *7.1.2 Revise little and often*

It is more effective and less stressful than cramming. You will also remember and understand more of a topic if you cover it three times in three separate one-hour slots than you will by spending three hours at one sitting on the same material. Remember: **spaced learning promotes retention and recall.**

### *7.1.3 Plan your method of revision*

Active revision is much more effective than passively reading through your notes and will help you to avoid the temptation simply to stare at your notes and textbooks, fooling yourself into thinking you are doing something useful. If you have taken advice given earlier in this guide then, overall, your work will be reasonably organized and summarized. If this is not the case, then your first task is to organize and summarize the material. Then you can start your active revision by constructing your own set of revision notes. Read a section of your notes/handouts/textbook(s). Ask yourself which are the key facts and concepts. Now put the book away and see if you can jot the key points down. Look for connections to other topics covered in both lectures and practicals.

#### *Revision cards*

Many people find it useful to summarize and condense topics progressively until the key information can be fitted onto a postcard. One side can list the main headings and sub-headings, and the other, simple diagrams and brief notes. Don't forget to include links to other topics. A collection of these cards provides you with a portable revision pack that can be used in bus queues, on the train, etc., as well as during more formal revision times.

#### *Spider diagrams or mind maps for revision*

An alternative to the use of cards is to generate a spider diagram or mind map to help you to revise. You need not limit your map to words – pictures can be added and these provide a powerful tool when trying to remember key elements of the topic while you are under examination conditions. Figure 7.1 shows a picture of a revision mind map with pictures. The map has been shrunk deliberately so that you cannot see the details, which don't matter. The important thing is to see what a difference a few key images and the imaginative use of colour can make. OK, for the very curious, the image in this case was revision notes based on the life and works of the poet Byron, who was "*mad, bad and dangerous to know*". Several computer programs can assist with this.

#### *Test yourself with practice questions once you have revised a topic*

For many examinations you can obtain copies of previous examination papers. These will give you a flavour of the type of questions that have been asked in the past. Tackling past examination papers will give you practice at writing examination answers. One of the best ways of doing this is to revise a topic, then attempt a past question under examination conditions. Allow yourself only 30 or 40 minutes to write down your answer, and do not refer to notes. When you have done this, look

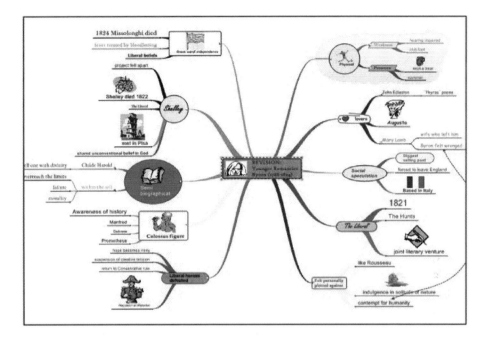

**Figure 7.1  A mind map with pictures to act as a revision aid**

at your answer, and see if it is structured well. You may like to refer back to "How to write a good essay" (*Section 5.5*) to judge this.

You should, however, treat past papers with a degree of caution. There may be questions that you could not possibly answer because courses evolve over time, and what was important in previous years may have been discarded to make room for new material. Furthermore, it may be that a member of staff who habitually used to ask questions on a particular topic is no longer working in the institution, and so this topic may no longer be taught in as much depth. Remember, however, great care is taken when setting examination papers to ensure that they are fair and that they cover the course at the time the examination is set. Your lecturers set the examinations, and have a detailed understanding of your curriculum so will set questions that should enable you to demonstrate your knowledge.

**An exercise to try**

Pick two questions that you consider you could answer equally well. Under time constraints typical for examinations (say 30 to 40 minutes) write out your answers to each. There is an additional rule. For one question you must start writing immediately. For the other you must **NOT** begin to write your essay for at least 5 minutes. During that time, however, you can formulate a plan of the outline of your essay. You may even like to make a spider diagram or mind map of things to include in your essay. Imagine that you had to mark your essays. Which approach produced the better answer? Which approach will you adopt in future?

## Group revision

Some people find that working in pairs or in small groups saves a lot of hard slog. The work can be shared out with people that you trust. Discuss outline answers to past questions and swap ideas. Explain topics to each other and compare answers to the same questions. How does your approach vary from that of your friends? If you can work in this way, you will find that you become good at assessing the quality of each others' work. It is also not an uncommon experience that students are often more critical in their judgement of one another than teachers are of their students.

## And finally....

1. Do not make worry a substitute for work.
2. Try to stay healthy – look after yourself.
3. Don't be complacent if you have moderate-to-good marks from the in-course work. You are in a good position, but a thorough understanding of the course will be important for future modules.

---

**Ten tips for avoiding pressure during revision**

1. Avoid stressful situations. Stress is contagious so don't moan to your friends about how much work you haven't done, or listen to people who tell you that they cannot sleep or that they are on tranquillizers.

2. Remember that you have a limited concentration span. Take short breaks every hour or so. Treat yourself. A short walk will refresh you as you realize that there is a world beyond the exam room.

3. When revising, test yourself to see how much you really do remember.

4. Don't drink lots of coffee or strong tea. Caffeine encourages adrenaline production and this induces stress. Tea has a lot of caffeine in it. Why not try herbal teas? (OK, because they can taste horrible.)

5. Don't turn into a recluse. The odd bit of socializing is good for you, providing you don't let it get out of control (see points 1 and 2).

6. Make sure you get enough sleep. Early nights are a good idea. Avoid burnout.

7. Don't leave all your revision to the last minute. Plan your work to build up steadily to the examination.

8. Don't make worry a substitute for work.

9. Try putting a few drops of perfume or aftershave on your wrists whilst revising. Do the same when you go in for your exam. Smell is a powerful memory trigger. It may work for you, too.

10. Stressed out? See your tutors. They are there to help you.

---

## 7.2 Examinations

### 7.2.1 *How to fail your exams*

**Method one:** do not write anything.

**Method two:** write everything you know about the topic mentioned in the exam question rather than selecting the appropriate information required by the exam question about that topic.

**Method three:** answer one question and get 100% for it and then ignore everything else. Simple arithmetic shows that if you have to answer three questions, then 100% + 0% + 0% = 33% overall mark. This is an automatic fail if 40% is the pass mark.

**Method four:** get out of your exam seat; go across to your best mate's place. Steal their paper and put your name on it. *But seriously...*

### 7.2.2 *Styles of exam*

## *Multiple choice questions (MCQs)*

They are commonly used because they can test a wide range of knowledge quickly and easily. In addition, they can be marked rapidly and objectively. They are efficient at testing factual knowledge. Skilful question-setters can adapt the MCQ format to test some aspects of problem-solving skills. If you use practice MCQ banks in revision, make sure that you understand why options are correct or incorrect, and appreciate how the question relates to the topic as a whole. **Do not try to remember hundreds of dissociated facts.** If you adopt a surface learning approach to MCQ exams, you are doomed to failure.

A variety of formats can be used for MCQ tests. In the simplest there is a root followed by a number of branches, only one of which is correct. For example:

Frogs are:

    A. always green (F)

    B. amphibians (T)

    C. warm blooded (F)

    D. feathered (F)

    E. hermaphrodite (F)

A variation of this is where only one branch is *in*correct.

Other question types, sometimes referred to as multiple response questions or MRQs, may adopt a flexible pattern in which students are required to select the correct responses to a particular root question, where there may be a number of possible options given and *at least one response* will be correct. For example:

Hormones:

    A. are structural molecules (F)

    B. are energy storage molecules (F)

    C. may be peptides (T)

    D. may be synthesized from cholesterol (T)

    E. are involved in endocrine signalling (T)

With certain types of MRQs, all responses may be correct. MRQs have a number of advantages for assessment at university, but there is also a significant problem: to score full marks, all a candidate needs to do is to mark every option as correct. To get around this, MRQ tests are subject to negative marking where, for each incorrect answer, the candidate has up to one full mark (or a fraction of a mark) deducted. The rationale for negative marking is to deter guesswork.

For the sake of brevity, in the text below, "MCQ" refers both to the strict multiple-choice format and to multiple-response questions.

**Strategies for passing MCQ tests:** you should read through the paper carefully and note all the responses you know to be false. These may often, but not always, contain words like *"which of the following never…"* and *"which of the following always…"*. Mark as correct those responses you know to be true. Now read through the paper again. This time go through each question very carefully. Remember that every word in a question will have been chosen with care, and that you can often get clues about what the examiner is trying to test from the nature of the root statement and the possible responses. On the second run through, weigh carefully the responses. If you are still uncertain about the truth of a response, on balance it is probably better to ignore it.

## Written examinations

Be well prepared and well rested for your exam. Last minute revision rarely pays off; most of the time it induces panic. If you have planned your studies and your revision using the advice in this book, you *will* have the knowledge to pass.

Try to take some time to relax the day before an examination and do not go to bed late. Aim to arrive at the examination hall in plenty of time, and find someone to talk to about topics other than the exam. Think positively. You will be nervous but so will everyone else. Continue to think positively. Take a few deep breaths and concentrate on relaxing tense muscles. A *mild*, controlled anxiety will enhance your performance and not detract from it. The trick is not to let the panic set in.

So, you are properly prepared, and you know you will pass. There are only three things that will stop you from passing now. These are:

- not reading the instructions
- not answering the questions
- not keeping to time

**Read the examination instructions carefully.** Make sure you understand the instructions and underline the key words. "*Answer <u>three</u> questions, <u>one</u> from <u>each</u> section*" means just that: answer **three** questions, answering **one question** in **each** of **three sections**. It does not mean "*answer all the questions on the paper*" nor "*answer any three questions*" nor "*answer the questions that you fancy answering*".

**Answer the questions properly.** Read through all the questions on the paper and turn over the paper to check whether there are any on the back. Carefully decide which questions you will tackle if you have a choice. If you do not have a choice of questions, start with the one that you feel most comfortable answering. Read through the question again, this time noting key phrases:

<u>Discuss</u>...
<u>Compare</u> and <u>contrast</u>...
<u>List</u>...
Write <u>short notes</u> on <u>three</u> of the following...

"*Discuss*" does not mean "*list*", nor does "*write short notes on...*" mean "*write a four page essay on...*"! Write an outline plan of your answer, as you did in your revision. It is a good idea to make your plan on the inside cover or first page of your answer book so that the examiners can see how you intend to tackle the question at a glance. If you do this, however, you should indicate clearly where the proper answer starts, particularly in answers for which you are invited to provide brief notes, which may get confused with your essay plan. For a half-hour question, your outline plan will take up five minutes or so, but it is time well spent. You are now ready to write a structured answer as discussed in *Section 5.5*. Make sure that your writing remains legible. Remember that your examiners need to read your words of wisdom.

Highlighted above are a few phrases that introduce questions and that cause students particular problems. There are many others. Table 7.1 lists some of the other common terms, together with a definition from the *Oxford English Dictionary* online, and additional notes if appropriate. You don't need to learn these by heart – just be aware of the various meanings when tackling questions in which they occur.

## Deductive questions

Deductive questions ask you to use your knowledge and problem-solving abilities to interpret and evaluate new information, which may be qualitative or quantitative. This type of question can be scary because it is less easy to understand quickly what sort of knowledge is needed and how it should be manipulated to reach the answer than in factual essay-type questions. Try not to be put off by this, however, because deductive questions usually have several parts that structure your thinking and guide you to what is required. Also, remember that these questions are designed to test the skills and knowledge that you have acquired during your course rather than anything that is far beyond its scope. To tackle deductive questions successfully you should read the given information carefully. Then, you should work out what the information means, i.e. interpret it, evaluate it and reach conclusions, or propose a hypothesis, according to what the question requires. A cool head and confidence are required to tackle deductive questions and these can be acquired with practice.

**Table 7.1 Analysis of common key terms used in examination questions**

| Term | *OED* definition | Notes |
|---|---|---|
| Analyse | To take to pieces; to separate, distinguish, or ascertain the elements of anything complex, as a material collection, chemical compound, light, sound, a miscellaneous list, account or statement, a sentence, phrase, word, conception, feeling, action, process, etc. | Examine in very close detail. Ask what the main features of the object are. Try to identify the principal points. |
| Assess | To evaluate (a person or thing); to estimate (the quality, value, or extent of), to gauge or judge. | Estimate the worth of the subject. Ask what the positive and negative points are. Consider whether views held by others on the subject are authoritative or not. |
| Comment on | To write explanatory or critical notes (*to*) *on*, or *upon* a text. | Identify the main topics of the subject and present your views based on your research to date. |
| Compare * | To mark or point out the similarities and differences of (two or more things); to bring or place together (actually or mentally) for the purpose of noting the similarities and differences. | To compare things you should show how two or more subjects are similar to one another. |
| Contrast * | To set in opposition (two objects of like nature, or one *with*, rarely *to*, another) in order to show strikingly their different qualities or characteristics, and compare their superiorities or defects. | To contrast two or more subjects you should point out the features in which the subjects differ from each other. You should indicate the criteria on which you base your judgement regarding these differences. |
| Define | To state precisely or determinately; to specify. | To define something you need to describe what you consider to be the exact meaning of the subject. |
| Describe | To set forth in words, written or spoken, by reference to qualities, recognizable features, or characteristic marks; to give a detailed or graphic account of. | To describe a subject you should set out the main features of that subject. |
| Discuss | To investigate or examine by argument; to sift the considerations for and against; to debate. | In discussion, you should set out the arguments for and against a proposition and draw your conclusions, indicating how these have been reached. |
| Distinguish | To make or draw a distinction; to perceive or note the difference between things; to exercise discernment; to discriminate. | When you are asked to distinguish between subjects you should highlight those features that make them different. |

| Term | *OED* definition | Notes |
|------|------------------|-------|
| Enumerate | To count, ascertain the number of; more usually, to mention (a number of things or persons) separately, as if for the purpose of counting; to specify as in a list or catalogue. | When enumerating subjects you should list them, often including a brief description of individual items. |
| Evaluate | *a.* Math. To work out the 'value' of (a quantitative expression); to find a numerical expression for (any quantitative fact or relation). *b.* gen. To 'reckon up', ascertain the amount of; to express in terms of something already known. | When asked to evaluate a subject you should assess and describe its worth. In evaluating propositions, there may be evidence in support and evidence that refutes the idea. In a good evaluation, you should include both types of evidence and make conclusions, indicating how these were reached. |
| Examine | To inquire or search into, investigate (a question or subject); to consider or discuss critically; to try the truth or falsehood of (a proposition, statement, *etc.*). | When examining a subject, you should consider it in detail. As part of this process, you may also wish to evaluate the subject critically. |
| Explain | To assign a meaning to, state the meaning or import of; to interpret. | When explaining something you need to demonstrate why the subject is the way that it is. |
| Illustrate | *a.* To shed light upon, light up, illumine. *b.* To throw the light of intelligence upon; to make clear, elucidate, clear up, explain. | When you are asked to illustrate a subject, you should make it clear and explicit. It helps if you can support your illustration with evidence as to why the subject is as it is. |
| Justify | To make good (an argument, statement, or opinion); to confirm or support by attestation or evidence; to corroborate, prove, verify. | If you are asked to justify an argument or proposition, you should provide the evidence in support of that idea, showing how the conclusions regarding the concept were reached. For contentious ideas, you may need to present evidence that is in contradiction to your argument. |
| Outline | To describe the broad outlines or main features of; to sketch in general terms, summarize. | In providing an outline, you should only describe the principal points of the subject, preferably as briefly as possible. |
| Review | *a.* To survey; to take a survey of. *b.* To write an appreciation or criticism of (a new literary work, a musical or dramatic performance, *etc.*) | In reviewing a subject you should describe its principal features, exploring the reasons why these are considered important. |
| Summarize | To make (or constitute) a summary of; to sum up; to state briefly or succinctly. | In summarizing a subject, you should draw out its principal points, omitting details and examples. Summaries are brief forms of outlines. |

*These are often combined. Sometimes you may be asked to compare two topics without being asked to contrast them. If you feel the need to show how they differ, state this explicitly.

### 7.2.3 Plan your time

Check the length of the exam, estimate how long you have for each question, and stick to it! Three hours to answer four questions allows 40 minutes per question, with twenty minutes to be split between the beginning and the end of the exam. This time is to read the questions before you start, and to check your answers at the end. Allocate time proportionally. The first 20% of marks are very easy to earn. The final 20% are the hardest marks to pick up. This is why you must attempt the required number of questions rather than relying on doing just two or three very well.

> ***Do not be tempted to spend a long time on your favourite topic at the expense of other questions.***

You are better off scoring 60%, 56% and 58%, giving an overall mark of 58% than you are scoring 80%, 60% and 20%, giving you an overall mark of 53.33%, just because you ran out of time on the last question.

# 7.3 What is looked for in an examination answer

Essays written under examination conditions cannot be as finely crafted as essays written in your own time at home, but there are many similarities in how they are assessed. The section below gives an idea of how different qualities of answer are graded.

## First class answer

This displays a complete understanding of the question. Nearly all of the information given in lectures, tutorials, etc. will be included, but there will also be evidence that you have read around the subject. Answers will be constructed from a variety of sources, logically organized, well presented, and substantially free from errors. If appropriate, the first class answer demonstrates originality of thought or approach and will also display insight.

## Upper second class answer

This is slightly less outstanding, but will display a sound understanding of the question, containing all, or nearly all of the information given in lectures as well as some evidence of reading around the subject, although not to the extent expected of first class answers. The answer will be largely error-free and will certainly not have any major errors of fact. It will be logically presented and the better answers in this class will demonstrate your ability to manipulate information.

## Lower second class answer

This is generally sound, repeating the material presented in lectures. It will probably not show evidence that you have read around the topic, but it will be free from major errors. The presentation will usually be less logical than answers deserving of higher classes.

## Third class answer

This provides evidence that you have some understanding of the question. Such answers are typically incomplete and may betray a poor appreciation of the subject.

Important points will not have been addressed and a third class answer may contain a quantity of irrelevant material. The presentation of such answers is generally poor.

## A pass mark or below

This answer must be a serious attempt, containing some relevant information to show that you have a limited understanding of the question. It will contain serious omissions or errors. If your answer is inadequate, lacking in substance or understanding then you will get a fail mark.

### 7.3.1 In-course assessments

A significant proportion of course marks may be gained through some form of in-course assessment rather than from examinations. The tasks that you will be set will vary from course to course, but you should be clear what proportion of the overall mark will be derived from in-course assessment, and how these marks can be earned. The important thing with in-course assessment is that you must **always hand something in**, no matter how badly you think you have done. You will never get less than zero for any piece of work attempted, and zero is all that you will get if you fail to hand work in, or if you do not turn up for a test. It is polite and also sensible to inform the person(s) running your courses if you are ill; they are more likely to be sympathetic and help you make up the work you missed, thereby allowing you to gain coursework marks you might otherwise have lost, than if you do nothing.

### 7.3.2 Summary of advice on examinations

If you want to succeed in your exams and do the best that you can, our top ten tips are given below.

---

**Checklist for examination success**

- Scan the paper to give yourself an idea of the scope and range of questions available.
- Make an initial selection of the questions you think you can do best. Don't worry if you don't think you can do the requisite number at this stage.
- Start with the question you think you can answer best.
- READ THE QUESTION PROPERLY.
- Draw up an answer plan (on your answer book cover is a good place). Ensure that you remain focused on the required information.
- Calculate how long you have per question/section and stick to the allotted time.
- Do answer the requisite number of questions even if you feel less confident of your last choice.
- If your mind goes blank then think about everything that you might know about a topic.
- If all else fails then try another question.
- *Remember*: the first 20% of marks are much easier to gain than the last 20% in any question.

### Good luck in your exams!

If you have read this section, it probably means that your exams are close. If so, let us hope that this is not the first time that you have opened this book!

# Chapter 8 Taking a year out

Some universities operate schemes that give students the opportunity to broaden their skills and experience by taking a year out of full-time study. This is usually, but not always, offered at the end of your second year. If available, this contributes in a positive manner to your degree. You may be able to undertake, for example, a placement in a relevant industry, a year studying at a foreign university, or voluntary work.

When you are making your decision about which university to attend, you should check which universities offer such schemes if you think that you would like to take a year out during your degree. Make sure that you also know what criteria are required to qualify for the scheme, such as the minimum level of academic achievement required to enrol on the programme, the relevance of any modules you are taking, and a timescale indicating what you must do in order to make your application. For example, if you are taking a year abroad in a country where English is not the first language, you will need to ensure that your language qualifications are suitable for the location in which you intend to study.

Departments where such schemes are well established are likely to have appropriate systems for helping students find a placement, and provide support while their students are away. They will also have tried-and-tested processes for coordinating with, and monitoring, the host organization. If the department does not normally run such schemes, you will need to gain appropriate permission and will also need to be prepared to do more of the basic work yourself to find suitable placement organizations and follow the relevant application procedures.

Some universities take account of your performance during the year out when calculating your final degree result, so you should check the assessment weighting and how this is applied. Other institutions regard the year out simply as a pass-or-fail year and, depending on your success, will indicate that you have been successful by awarding you a degree with a title that recognizes your achievement.

Work that can be done during the vacations does not normally require permission from your university but can be equally valuable in providing useful experiences and helping you to develop relevant skills.

## 8.1 Why bother? The pros and cons of taking a year out

So, why bother prolonging the time it will take for you to gain your degree? Daunting though a year out may seem at the start of your undergraduate journey, there are many reasons why you should consider the matter seriously.

Both an industrial placement and a study year abroad will broaden your experience of life by presenting new and interesting challenges. The activities you undertake during this additional year may also give you a firmer idea of what sort of career you might prefer and where in the world you might like to work. While on these schemes, you will meet and work with new groups of people, experience a different environment, work to different timetables and, if you choose to study abroad, you will encounter a different culture, and perhaps be required to communicate in a different language. In the global economy, this will be a valuable asset in your search for future employment.

On a personal level, you will develop a greater degree of self-reliance, become more efficient at managing your activities and time, become a better communicator through your interaction with a variety of different people, and will be able to use your initiative to deal with different sets of circumstances and problems. These skills will be recognized by any future employers and are likely to give you an advantage when applying for jobs. You might also make useful contacts to whom you might apply for a job later in life.

There are direct benefits of the year out in terms of your studies and future employment. First, most students come back to university more confident and more self-assured – as well as one year older of course – and this additional maturity usually stands them in good stead when addressing their final year studies. They often end up with very good degrees. Then, of course, the year out experience is valuable additional material for your *curriculum vitae* (CV) when applying for that first job, and will typically place you at a distinct advantage in the graduate jobs market.

Taking a year out means that some of the peer group with whom you started your course will have left by the time you return to your academic studies. In reality, some of your peer group will probably also have taken a year out and will return to university studies when you do. So when you start your final year you will have a nice mix of old and new friends.

Finally, having a year out may have a major impact on your financial situation because, in addition to living expenses and accommodation, you may be required to pay a proportion of the university fees. However, many industrial placements offer a salary that will cover living expenses and accommodation throughout the year, and some students even manage to pay off some long-standing debts! A year at a university abroad or of voluntary work, however, may leave you seriously out of pocket, and you should investigate the possibility of obtaining a bursary or sponsorship as a means of supporting yourself in these circumstances.

## 8.2  An industrial year out

When applying for an industrial placement, you will be in competition with students from around the country, as would happen if you were applying for a normal job. It is vital that you complete an appropriate application form and submit a suitable up-to-date CV. Your departmental tutor will need to write you a reference indicating your suitability for a placement, which may also require approval by the university. If you are invited for interview, you must give the best impression you can to your interviewers. If you are then offered a placement, it is your responsibility to make the most of the opportunity.

A major benefit of working in a research setting is the opportunity to gain a range of subject-specific technical skills and to use the latest research techniques and equipment. Another benefit is that you will be conducting meaningful research that may even lead to a research publication that can be listed on your CV. You will also be able to experience the group dynamics and teamwork required for successful research environments. For many students, the experience of an industrial year out is also very helpful in helping them decide whether they would like to move into research after completing their degree – at least to PhD level and possibly even moving on to an industrial career thereafter. At the end of the placement, most students write a report and may produce a presentation such as a poster or a mini-seminar, so good communication and presentation skills will be important here.

You may be uncertain about whether you will have lost the habit of academic working during a year out and how much academic material you have forgotten, and may believe that integrating back into your university course will be difficult. This is (almost) never a problem. Much more common is to find that the extra year's maturity helps students to focus more effectively on their end goal – to get the best possible degree. You may actually find that the relevance of the academic material becomes clearer having done a year of 'real-life' science. The following sections offer suggestions on how to derive most benefit from the year in an industrial placement.

### 8.2.1 *How to make a success of your industrial placement*

Successful placements require a very high level of commitment and you should work hard and behave in a professional manner at all times. This means that you should show an interest in the project you are given, be enthusiastic about the tasks involved, and be prepared to put in appropriate hours to get a job done. It is important that you ask questions to make sure you understand what is required of you and that you can show some initiative and work independently. The more expertise and reliability you can show, the more your project leader is likely to trust you to take on more advanced and, quite likely, more interesting work using a greater variety of techniques. This will help you to develop your practical skills further. Make the most of working as part of a group by observing and learning how the other team members deal with issues that arise. You will meet a variety of people and have an opportunity to talk with many about their roles and what career paths led them to that position. This may give you ideas for the future, but also, importantly, you may decide to ask one of them for a future reference.

Help yourself settle in quickly by making the most of the social opportunities on offer; there may be a sports centre and organized activities that you can join. If there are other students on industrial placements at the same company, see if you can share a flat together – you are all in the same boat and can share your experiences.

Many universities ensure that your industrial supervisor is given clear guidelines on the project type and supervision that needs to be provided and there will often be an Industrial Work Profile to be completed by the student and industrial supervisor during the course of the year. This will describe skills acquired, work done, goals achieved, etc. Typically you will remain in contact by email and telephone with your university during your year out and an academic tutor from your university may well visit the company site to meet with you and your supervisor and check that all is well.

Problems may arise if your expectations do not match with the position you are given within the placement. It is possible that the company is assessing your abilities before moving you on to working in a more responsible situation, but if things don't improve within a few weeks it is important that you talk to your industrial supervisor and your University tutor so you can sort it out. If you are not enjoying the work, again, you must find someone to talk to about this; you may have unrealistic expectations of the work, or you might be allowed to swap the focus of the work to something you find more enjoyable.

In the event of a personality clash with your supervisor, you might need to call upon all your energies to maintain a professional relationship. Again, however, it is worthwhile talking to your university tutor and to others working in the team; they may be able to give moral support and advice especially if they have a similar relationship issue with the supervisor. If difficulties persist, you should approach the Human Resources section of your place of work as it is their job to address such issues.

Finally, do **not** expect to have a successful industrial placement if you:

- spend a lot of time socializing
- make a lot of mistakes
- waste time
- turn up late for work
- appear uninterested
- fail to show initiative
- ignore the other group members

This will create a very bad impression and may endanger the chances of any other student from your university obtaining a placement there in the future.

### Checklist for a successful industrial placement

- Be committed to the work – be prepared to work the required hours to get the job done.
- Act professionally.
- Show enthusiasm.
- Ask questions if you do not understand anything.
- Develop your practical skills.
- Complete the industrial work profile as you progress through the year.
- Learn from others in the team.
- Join in with social activities.

# 8.3  Study year abroad

You may be attracted to a study year abroad because you are interested in discovering more about a particular culture and/or you would like to improve your language ability whilst continuing your academic studies. Opportunities exist for students to visit a variety of places throughout the world such as the USA, the Far East, or even Australia. The Erasmus scheme applies to students studying at European universities. Taking a study year abroad involves spending a year in a foreign university, attending courses and, most likely, conducting a project in an established research group. To ensure parity between the academic standards in your home university and the institution you visit, your home university will already have checked that a suitable range of courses at the correct level is available for visiting students. In addition to modules in your subject area, there are likely to be modules covering a very different range of topics from those offered in the UK; for example, in Singapore, you may be offered Islam in Contemporary Malay Society, and in the USA modules covering the History of Black African Women in Society have been offered.

To qualify for the scheme you will be required to make an application and to obtain a reference from one of your tutors. Universities often have well-established links with particular institutions abroad, so there is less likely to be competition for those places from students from other universities, than when students are competing for industrial placements.

By opting for a study year abroad you will be continuing your academic studies in a different culture and also possibly in a different language. Integrating into a student group with a very different culture can be daunting, but if successful, will bring great rewards, as illustrated by the comments from a student who spent a year in Singapore:

> *"I was very lucky to enjoy the support and friendship of a close-knit lab who introduced me to the Singaporean life, especially the wonderful array of food! I was invited to take part in a traditional Chinese wedding ceremony, which was a highlight of my time there. Other foreign students came from numerous other countries and I now have friends in Canada, America, Europe, China, Australia and many more. ...It was an amazing opportunity which I would repeat in a flash."*

## 8.3.1  *How to make a success of your study year abroad*

In many ways, the recommendations for a successful industrial placement also apply to a study year abroad. It is important to be committed, that you attend all the teaching sessions, and spend an appropriate time working on your project. You will be interacting with a research group in a similar manner to students on the industrial placement, so it is very important to give a good impression especially if you might want to return to work there in the future. Although it may be difficult to break into friendship groups that are already established, especially if there is a language barrier, there are bound to be societies and clubs through which you can establish a circle of friends. If you have learned much more about the culture of the country you visit and have made new friends by the time you return to the UK, you will have fulfilled a large part of the aims of a study year abroad scheme.

It could be very easy to feel isolated in a foreign country, especially if you find it hard to get to know other students. If this feeling continues for more than a few weeks, it is VERY important to talk to somebody. Your project supervisor or someone else at the University who is involved in organizing the visits is a good place to start. You must also let your tutor at home know (by email) how you are feeling because they can offer advice and contact relevant people at the institution where you are. The VERY WORST THING you can do is to bottle up your feelings and not tell anyone. If you discover one of the modules you have chosen is not what you expected, you should ask if it is possible to change to a different one – and keep your tutor at home informed of what you are doing. For a very few students, problems such as this can lead to depression, poor attendance, and possibly a failure to complete the year. Remember the advice we have already given on asking for help.

---

### Checklist for a successful year abroad

- Attend all the required teaching sessions.
- Show enthusiasm for your project.
- Ask questions if you do not understand something.
- Show initiative and independence where appropriate.
- Be prepared to work the required hours to get your work completed.
- Be aware that although you may feel isolated at first, this feeling is likely to pass soon.
- If a feeling of isolation continues TALK TO SOMEONE ABOUT IT.
- Make new friends by joining societies and clubs.
- Explore the country and the culture.

# Chapter 9 Your final year

If you have followed the advice in this book, eventually, and this will happen sooner than you may think possible, you will enter your final year. After that, you will have to face the big bad world. To make sure that you are properly prepared, you should plan to make the most of the opportunities open to you. One of the key features of your final year is your project. You will also need to prepare for the world beyond the ivory towers of Academe. This section provides advice on optimizing your performance in your final level of study.

## 9.1 Final year projects

In your final year, you will probably carry out a research project. This involves considerable effort each week. Like practicals, projects may or may not be laboratory-based. A project that is not laboratory-centred may involve, for example, the preparation and presentation of a dissertation, exploring important topical questions. This requires assembly and critical reading of previously published research papers. As such, much of this type of project may be library-based. Another popular format for such so-called "dry" projects is to undertake a survey. Some students prepare education and information packs and even film storyboards, communicating scientific ideas to a lay audience; others plan applications for research grants. Alternatively, projects may entail the development of a particular type of computer software. The only limit on this type of project is your imagination.

Laboratory projects involve tinkling the glassware (these days, however, glass has largely been replaced with plastic!). They demand that students undertake individual practical research projects under supervision. Such projects will typically be carried out in the research laboratory run by the project supervisor, instead of in large teaching laboratories. This gives students the opportunity to work alongside research students and technicians, from whom they can learn a great deal.

As in all other areas of your undergraduate work, for success in your final year project you will need to be strategic, to plan, to be diligent in following your plan, and to present your project clearly. Regardless of the type of project, you must first identify the aims of the project: what is the problem and what are you trying to achieve? From this you must identify the tasks that need to be done to achieve the aims, including the objectives and any methods or approaches that it will be useful to follow – the published literature will help in this. Set yourself a feasible timescale but also be flexible to allow for unexpected avenues of research. Your results must be clearly presented, with your conclusions related to both the project aims and the current accepted understanding of the project topic in the literature. Finally, the whole must be succinctly presented in a report that conforms to the subject's academic style. Ensure that you do not become 'sloppy' as this will affect the final product.

Whatever type of project you undertake, you will be acquiring many skills that will be of great benefit in your future career. These include planning and organizing your time, developing a critical approach to published material, and learning how to present your findings in the most appropriate manner.

# 9.2 Planning for life after university: thinking about careers

Sooner or later, the day will come when you will venture out into the world of work and get a job. Some of you will be glad of the opportunity to earn a salary and to support yourself as soon as you have finished your degree; others, no doubt, will delay this event and choose to continue in higher education, aspiring to a higher degree. For both groups, success will come to those who have clear plans, and the strategy for securing a good job is the same as the strategy that is most likely to secure a top PhD position. There are numerous sources of help, support and advice but, ultimately, the only person who can make appropriate decisions regarding your future is you. The more carefully you plan for your future, the more likely you are to succeed. This section is intended to give advice on a strategy to adopt.

### 9.2.1 *Gather information*

Some students have a very clear desire to follow a particular career path after their first degree; others have little idea what they want to do. Whichever group you belong to, the most important first step to securing a successful career is to get as much information as possible about what is available to you. This includes informing yourself of several alternatives so that, should things not work out for you, you have something to fall back on.

### 9.2.2 *Assess your skills and qualifications*

Employers often draw up lists of essential attributes and desired attributes when seeking to employ graduates, so if you don't have any of the essential attributes, even just one, you will be wasting your time putting in an application. Therefore, the next step in successful career planning is to assess whether you have the necessary skills and aptitudes for the jobs that interest you; it is very important to take a critical look at your abilities, strengths and weaknesses. It may be easy to identify abilities and strengths but it can be hard looking at your weaknesses. Unless you are honest with yourself and recognize your limitations, you will apply for positions that are unsuitable for you and you will end up with a long string of rejections, which is very demoralizing. You should also focus on your interests and motivations. A well-paid job that bores you rigid may be tolerable for a few weeks or months, but it is no basis on which to build a successful career.

### 9.2.3 *Make a short list of available jobs*

Having decided on what interests you, and whether you have the necessary attributes and qualifications, the next step is to find out what is available. Your university Careers Service will undoubtedly provide a rich source of information. The jobs sections in newspapers and in scientific journals, such as *Nature* and *New Scientist*, are very good sources of information. In addition, you may find jobs advertised on the internet. It is often surprising just how many jobs are on offer each week and the range of jobs for science graduates is astonishing so, hopefully, you should find some that appeal to you. You should then make a short list of those to which you want to apply.

### 9.2.4 *Make the most of first contacts*

Sometimes, employers give contact details for applicants to discuss posts before making a formal application. This is always worthwhile; if nothing else, it shows that you have an interest in the position being advertised. Even though such contact is generally informal, it is an opportunity to sell yourself and thorough preparation will pay dividends. If there is a telephone number to contact, do your homework: find out as much as you can about your potential employer and use this information to frame a list of pre-prepared questions. It is essential that you understand the nature of the job for which you apply; failure to do so could leave you in a job in which you soon become very unhappy. If applying for a PhD position, read the publications from the lab to which you want to apply. Remember that it is probably **not** a good idea to start with questions focusing on the social side of the job! If the contact involves a visit, make sure you dress appropriately; managers of field centres rarely wear high heels to work.

### 9.2.5 *Your* curriculum vitae

While the prospect of finding a job may seem a long way off when you are new to university, planning can never start too soon. In parallel with your PDP, it is a good idea to draft your CV at a very early opportunity. If you plan to take a year in industry, you will need to prepare a CV very soon into your undergraduate career, but even if this does not appeal to you, the earlier you draft a CV, the better. If you keep this as an electronic file, it becomes a relatively trivial task to keep it updated with significant milestones during your academic career. The earlier you start, the more time you will have to produce a CV of which you can be proud.

A CV is a document listing your personal details, and includes a history of your education, your qualifications and achievements, and other information such as your interests. Your prospective employer(s) will invariably want to see one in order to assess how suitable you will be for their job. Your PDP will help you to remember the important events that occurred to you at university, and will also be invaluable if you are asked questions about how you developed your skills and attributes throughout the course and what skills you might bring to the job.

### Creating a CV

Since employers will gain the first impression of you through your CV, it is **vital** that you present it in the best possible format; a poorly presented CV indicates that you are either unable or cannot be bothered to make an effort, and your application is likely to be directed straight into the waste paper basket! Remember, also, to tailor your CV to fit each job for which you apply since each one is likely to request slightly different attributes and skills. Things to remember are:

- keep the information well spaced with important details clearly visible
- include information that is relevant to the job and do not include irrelevant information
- keep your language simple and to the point
- avoid any unexplained time gaps in your education or employment; it is better to be up-front about gaps in a CV than to ignore them or, worse, try to cover them up
- ALWAYS check the grammar and spelling (use a dictionary)
- ask a friend to look over and comment on your drafts
- expect to have to redraft the CV several times before you achieve the final result
- use a simple font such as Arial or Times New Roman, rather than something more casual such as Comic Sans or fancy such as *Monotype Corsiva*
- use good quality paper (white) and a high-resolution printer

## What to include in your CV

- Your personal information: your name, address, contact telephone numbers and email address. Remember to make sure your email address does not give the wrong impression: as before, 'studmuffin' or 'sexy_babe' are not appropriate!
- Previous education: in chronological order starting with the most recent.
- Any work experience: list everything in chronological order from the most recent – make sure the dates you give are precise.
- Other skills and qualifications: such as a driving licence, first aid training, special ability in languages, musical and sports qualifications, or leadership and organizational skills that might be highlighted by particular activities in which you have engaged.
- Your interests and activities: anything that shows you have more qualities than can be ascertained from your education and previous employment.
- Referees and their contact details: it is usual to be asked for two; ideally one of your tutors and, if possible, one from an employer, although if you have not had work experience, two different academic referees can be listed. Do remember to get permission from them before listing them on your CV.

### 9.2.6 Making an application

Once you have got this far, you are ready to make your application. Take care with your presentation and answer all the questions on your application honestly. If you are caught not telling the truth, the consequences could blight the rest of your career. Indeed, it has been suggested that you could lay yourself open to prosecution for fraud. If asked to supply a CV with your application, make sure it is well presented: be careful in your choice of fonts, colours and paper. Stencil script in pale green on lilac paper will certainly stand out from the crowd, but will it really convey a message that most employers want to receive? Likewise, take care over any covering letter that you use to accompany your application. This should be short: ideally no more than one side of A4 paper. It gives you the opportunity to explain, succinctly, why you feel that you are particularly suited to the job and also allows you to explain any potential problem areas on your CV, like the poor marks you got for certain modules. If you follow this advice, then invitations to interviews will start piling up. Again, preparation is the key and if you have prepared properly, then the job offers will soon follow.

Future employers and PhD supervisors will usually require two references about you so your CV should contain the name and contact details of two referees. If you are applying for employment, one referee should be able to comment on your recent academic studies and the other should ideally have some experience of your performance in the workplace, to provide comments about your employability skills and attributes. A good choice of academic referee would be someone who knows you well such as your personal tutor or your project supervisor. As mentioned above, it is polite to contact your chosen referees to ask if they are willing to act in this way for you. To write an effective reference for a specific post they need to know the specifications of the job you are applying for. Try to make the work easy for them by sending these details rather than simply referring them to a website. It is also useful to let them see your proposed letter of application or personal statement to help them to focus their reference. They may also be able to make useful suggestions on content. Ensure that you and your referees are clear about how the reference is to be communicated; some PhD application processes require you to enclose written references with your application, others ask the referee to contact them directly and some companies may expect email or telephone references.

### 9.2.7  The 'milk round'

Graduates are sought after by employers. By the time you graduate, you will have acquired and practised numerous 'transferable skills' that make you useful to employers in the sciences and beyond. In recognition of this, large companies organize themselves to visit selected campuses for the purpose of recruitment in events known as the 'milk round'. If your university participates in this scheme you will have the opportunity to discover more about the companies in which you are interested and may even be offered on-the-spot interviews. If you are unsure about what career you might like, this is an ideal opportunity to gather information from all the employers attending by talking to the staff manning the stands. You might then be able to refine your ideas.

# 9.3  Be prepared for opportunities when they arise

Whatever career you decide to pursue, the take-home message from this section is that success will come with good preparation. Find out as much as you can about yourself, your aspirations and motivations and do the same about your potential employers. A final piece of advice is to keep an open mind. Circumstances sometimes close off options but this should be seen as an opportunity rather than a threat. If you find that for any reason you cannot follow the career path that you had planned, be prepared to explore alternatives. These can be very rewarding if approached with a positive attitude.

# Appendices for *Office 2007*

These appendices describe the efficient use of the *Word, Excel* and *PowerPoint* programs that form part of the *Microsoft Office* package. There are currently two versions of the *Office* package in common use:

- *Office 2003* for *Windows XP* (sometimes found running on *Vista* too)
- *Office 2007* for *Windows (XP* and *Vista)*

The Appendices in this book provide guidance on the use of *Office 2007*. However, if you use *Office 2003*, please go to www.scionpublishing.com/studyingscience where you will find another set of Appendices (as pdf files) describing that version of the software.

# Appendix A:
# Working well with *Word*

*Word* is the word processing package in the *Microsoft Office* suite. It has a wide range of functions that may be used to create a variety of formats for documents, to produce a range of text sizes, styles and fonts, and to create tables within documents. It can also check for mistakes in spelling and grammar. You are already very likely to be familiar with some of these facilities, so this section will not dwell on the basic mechanisms of word processing in detail. Instead, its aims are:

- to help you to increase your efficiency by introducing some faster ways of doing the basic operations
- to explain how you can produce more polished and professional-looking documents by helping you to explore some of the less obvious functions of the software

If you want to dip into different sections of the appendices without reading it all the way through, do make sure you first understand the notation used. This is described in *Section A1.2* and refers to *Word 2007,* usually found with *Windows Vista* operating system.

## A1  Menus, ribbons and toolbars

Functions in *Word* can be accessed via several routes, though as we shall see, the most familiar methods are not necessarily the quickest. The most general method is through the Tabbed Main Menu (Figure A1), positioned across the top of the screen:

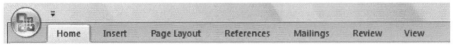

**Figure A1  The Tabbed Main Menu**

Left-clicking (using a right-handed mouse)[2] on any one of these words enables you to see its associated ribbon that appears immediately below the menu, and then you can select any function in that ribbon by clicking on its icon. Some facilities may only be available from 'Dialogue Boxes' or 'Menus', which are reached after a series of further steps. For example, creating SMALL CAPITAL letters requires a click over a button in the 'Font' group of the 'Home' ribbon to make the 'Font' dialogue box available and from this the small capitals option can then be chosen.

---

2 Right-clicking when using a left-handed mouse.

If you forget what individual icons on the toolbars do, point the mouse cursor ▷ at any icon *without* pressing any mouse button and you will see a small label appear (the tool tip), which describes the function of that icon.

If you want more space on the screen, you can make the ribbon disappear by double-clicking over the name of its tab in the Tabbed Main Menu. To make it reappear, double-click on the relevant tab name. You can make the ribbon appear temporarily by clicking once on the tab; it will disappear with the next click of the mouse.

## A1.1 *The Quick Access Toolbar*

As you work, it is likely that you will require functions in the different ribbons such as undoing or redoing an operation, while inserting images or adding references to a document, before saving and printing. To speed up this process you can make some of the most commonly used functions available, much more conveniently, through the 'Quick Access' toolbar (Figure A2). This can easily be created across the top of the screen and it will be visible regardless of the ribbon you are using. By clicking on the Office Button 🔘 at the top left-hand corner of the screen, choosing '*Word Options*' (at the bottom of the menu) and then '*Customize*', you can see the 'Customize Quick Access Toolbar and keyboard shortcuts' dialogue box. Within this dialogue box you can select the functions you want to appear in the 'Quick Access' toolbar. The '*Choose commands from*' option allows you to select functions from different tabs. An alternative way of accessing this dialogue box is to click on the little down-arrow on the right of the Office Button and select '*More Commands*'. An illustration of a Quick Access toolbar containing a variety of useful functions is shown in Figure A2.

**Figure A2  The Quick Access toolbar**

## A1.2 *The notation used*

In all three appendices in this section of the book (describing use of *Word*, *PowerPoint* and *Excel*, respectively), functions that are accessible through the buttons, menus and ribbons will conventionally be shown in italics, with the button, menu and ribbon choices separated by slashes (/). So, for example, the 'Save As' function will be shown as: '*Office Button/Save As*'. Do remember in what follows, however, that these functions can often be accessed more speedily by the alternative means described below.

# A2 General time-saving tips

## A2.1 *Shortcut menus and the right mouse button*[3]

You can greatly reduce the time you spend word processing if you understand how to use the right mouse button. While the left button of the mouse is most frequently used for selecting text or functions such as those on the menus or ribbons, pressing the *right* button allows you to 'shortcut' to some operations so you do not need to go through the Tabbed Menu and its various ribbons. Place the cursor in the appropriate position, or select the part of a document you want to change (information on how to select is covered in *Section A2.3*) then 'right-click' the mouse, and a menu will appear that is likely to contain the function you wish to apply. If you get used to trying this, you will soon learn which functions are available in this way and are likely to discover that it is much quicker than having to find the relevant ribbon and click on the appropriate icon.

## A2.2 *Shortcut key combinations*

Another way of speeding up your word processing – especially if you are able to touch-type – is by using combinations of keys (holding down two or more keys simultaneously) to obtain specific functions, rather than using the mouse. This can save a great deal of time, avoiding the need to move the mouse to the top of the screen and possibly to progress through several different menus, ribbons, or dialogue boxes before arriving at the facility you want. There are many different key combinations you could use, and some of the more useful ones are shown in Table A1. With time and practice you will gradually begin to remember those that are most useful to you, and may well start using them in preference to the menus and ribbons.

The key combinations in the right-hand columns of Table A1 give direct shortcuts to a particular function, as explained at the bottom of the table. Additional key combinations are shown in the left-hand column for the file-associated shortcuts. These are particularly useful when there is no direct shortcut combination to a facility[4]. With these shortcuts the underlined character must be held down simultaneously with the '**Alt**' key to take you to the required option. For example, there is no direct shortcut for '*Word*'s '*Save As*' function but it can be selected from the keyboard by activating the Office Button in *Word 2007* (similar to the '*File*' menu in previous versions of *Word*) using '**Alt+F**', i.e. holding down the '**Alt**' key while you type the '**F**' key and then selecting the 'Save As' item within that menu using '**Alt+A**'. So, *Word*'s '*Save As*' function can be selected from the keyboard with '**Alt+F**' then '**Alt+A**'. Note that activating some facilities such as the 'Font' dialogue box, represented in the text by '*Home/Font*', where two letters in a single word are underscored, you must hold down the '**Alt**' key and press in order '**H**' then '**F**' then '**N**' ('**Alt+H/Alt+F+N**').

---

3 For a left-handed mouse, reverse the 'handedness'.
4 These were devised using earlier versions of *Word* where the functions were organized in a different manner from *Word 2007*, with distinct 'File' and 'Edit' menus, and the keys used reflect the names of the original menus. For simplicity of presentation, Table A1 groups them accordingly.

**Table A1  Shortcut key combinations**

| Shortcuts | Key combination | Shortcuts | Key combination |
|---|---|---|---|
| File associated (via the Office Button) | | Formatting | |
| *Office Button/New* | Ctrl+N | *Format/Change Case* | Shift+F3 |
| *Office Button/Open* | Ctrl+O | Small capitals | Ctrl+Shift+K |
| *Office Button/Close* | Ctrl+W | Subscript | Ctrl+= |
| *Office Button/Save* | Ctrl+S | Superscript | Ctrl+Shift+= |
| *Office Button/ W/Print Preview* | Ctrl+F2 | Apply heading 1 | Alt+Ctrl+1 |
| | | Apply heading 2 | Alt+Ctrl+2 |
| *Office Button/Print* | Ctrl+P | Apply heading 3 | Alt+Ctrl+3 |
| *Office Button/Exit* | Alt+F4 | Apply list bullet | Ctrl+Shift+L |
| | | Make bold/not bold | Ctrl+Shift+B |
| **Editing** | | Italicize/unitalicize | Ctrl+Shift+I |
| Undo | Ctrl+Z | **Miscellaneous** | |
| Redo | Ctrl+Y | Go to start of document | Ctrl+Home |
| Cut | Ctrl+X or Shift+Delete | Go to end of document | Ctrl+End |
| Copy | Ctrl+C or Ctrl+Insert | End of line extend | Shift+End |
| Paste | Ctrl+V or Shift+Insert | Delete (rest of) word | Ctrl+Delete |
| Select All | Ctrl+A | Delete previous bit of word | Ctrl+Backspace |
| Find | Ctrl+F | Insert page break | Ctrl+Return |
| Replace | Ctrl+H | Next misspelling | Alt+F7 |
| Go To | Ctrl+G | Thesaurus | Shift+F7 |

'Ctrl+N' means *'hold down the* 'Ctrl' *key while typing* 'N', *then release it'* etc.
'Return' means the 'Enter' or ⏎ key; 'Backspace' means the ⟵ key

Reminders of most of these shortcut combinations can be seen both within the menus and also in the explanations given by the tool tip. For example the tool tip for 'Paste' in 'Home' ribbon shows the shortcut **'Ctrl+V'** and that for 'Bold' as **'Ctrl+B'**. In addition, the shortcut keys for each of the tabs in the Tabbed Menu (and also the 'Quick Access' toolbar) appear when you depress the **'Alt'** key once, and if you then click the appropriate **'Alt+key'** combination for a tab when its ribbon is on view (for example, clicking **'Alt+H'** when the 'Home' ribbon is on display) all the shortcut keys for individual functions within that ribbon are displayed. Do remember, however, that it is the *sequence* of the shortcuts that defines their function, so using **'Alt+C'** directly after **'Alt+F'** will produce a different effect from **'Alt+C'** directly after **'Alt+E'**. If you take note of these reminders whenever you use any of the menu options, you should gradually begin to remember the key combinations.

## A2.3  Selecting parts of a document for bulk operations
If you hold down the left mouse button and move (drag) the cursor over a piece of text (or a diagram, a picture, etc.), that portion of the document will become

highlighted `like this` to show that it has been selected. Another way of selecting a chunk of text, which can be more convenient if the chunk occupies more than one screen, is to click at one end of it then 'Shift-click' (i.e. hold down the **'Shift'** key while clicking the left mouse button) at the other end. The selected section can then be manipulated as you wish; for example, it can be deleted or copied or its font can be changed.

Performing the same function on several different chunks of a document simultaneously is easy because you can select them all first and then apply the required operation just once. To select more than one chunk, hold down the **'Ctrl'** key *after* you have made the first selection and keep holding this key down until all the subsequent selections have been made. This handy technique is called 'Ctrl-clicking', and works similarly in other *Office* applications, so it is well worth remembering. The same is true of 'Shift-clicking', mentioned in the previous paragraph.

### A2.3.1  Moving and duplicating whole chunks of document

You can move whole sections of documents to a different place by first selecting them, then positioning the cursor over a selected portion, before depressing the left mouse button. The button must remain depressed while you move, or 'drag', the highlighted section to a new position before it is finally released. This is called 'dragging and dropping'.

If, instead, you want to duplicate the selected portion in another part of the document, you can do this by holding down the Ctrl key while you drag the portion to the appropriate position. This is a much faster way of copying sections to different places than using alternatives such as the shortcut menu or even the or the **'Ctrl+C/ Ctrl+V'** sequence of operations.

### A2.3.2  Beware of inadvertently deleting selected sections

Selecting a section of the document and then immediately pressing almost ANY key will automatically delete the selected portion[5], so once you've made a selection, be careful not to type carelessly. The advantage of this behaviour is that when making a correction to your text, you do not need to spend time deleting a highlighted portion before typing in the corrected text; you can simply highlight the old text and then type your replacement.

### A2.4  The Clipboard(s)

The *Windows* Clipboard provides a temporary storage area for up to 24 items of text, pictures, etc. and you can see what you have stored in the 'Clipboard' task pane by clicking on the little arrow at the bottom of the 'Clipboard' group in the 'Home' ribbon. Selected text, pictures, diagrams, etc. can be removed to the

---

5  This behaviour can be changed, using **'Alt+F'** which takes you to the *'Office Button'*. From there use *'Windows Options'* to select *'Advanced'* and within this, deselect *'Typing replaces selected text'*. It is worth bearing in mind that much of *Word*'s behaviour can be modified through *'Windows Options'* in the *'Advanced'*, *'Customize'* and *'Proofing'* menus. Here, however, we shall usually assume, for simplicity, that *Word* is operating in its standard 'default' manner.

clipboard by 'cutting' them out using **'Ctrl+X'** (or '*Cut*' in the shortcut menu), or by copying them to the clipboard using **'Ctrl+C'** (or '*Copy*' in the shortcut menu). Material stored in the clipboard can be inserted into any document (or transferred into another *Windows* application) using **'Ctrl+V'** or the shortcut menu. The task pane can also be used if you want to paste earlier clipboard contents. You can remove material from the 'Clipboard' task pane by right-clicking on it and choosing the '*Delete*' command.

## A2.5 The Insert key

The **'Insert'** key, pressed once, causes new text to 'overwrite', while pressing it a second time returns it to its previous state. This can be useful if you want to change specific parts of the text quickly, but if you start to overwrite (i.e. you find that what you're typing is obliterating the existing text, instead of being inserted before it), then you may have pressed the **'Insert'** key by mistake and will need to press it again to correct this.

## A2.6 Moving around a document

You can move around a document in several ways.

- Using the scroll bars to the right of the screen or the up- and down-arrow keys to move line by line.
- Using the **'Page Up'** and **'Page Down'** keys to move page by page.
- Creating a split screen via '*View/Split*' so that your document appears in both screens, with independent scroll bars so you can see two different parts of the document simultaneously. This is very useful when needing to refer to and edit sections that are distant from each other.
- Creating an extra window showing your document via '*View/New Window*' so that you can move independently through each screen. (Note: if you need to see more than one document simultaneously, the '*View/Arrange Window*' provides this option.)
- Using a Document Map ('*View/Document Map*', or **'Alt+W/Alt+V+M'**) which shows the main features (headings, figures, etc.) that have been formatted using the '*Styles*' function (explained in *Section A3.3*). This is particularly useful if you want to keep the structure of a long document, such as a Level 3 project, in view while you are working on it. Clicking on a feature will take you straight to that part of the document. Right-clicking over the Document Map activates a menu which allows you to choose the level of detail of the map so, for example, you can look at the overall structure using 'Show Heading 1' (the main section headings), then increase the detail, perhaps to 'Show Heading 3', to find the particular sub-section you want. You can also expand or collapse each section using the '+' and '−' symbols next to each heading.
- Using the Outline View ('*View/Outline*', or **'Alt+W/Alt+U'**), which, like the Document Map, displays headings that have been formatted using the '*Styles*'

facility. By changing the 'Level' setting you can expand or collapse the document, which provides a very quick way of finding, and editing, the text of specific sections. While working in Outline View it is very easy to reorganize sections of a document by dragging and dropping selected sections up or down the list. The 'Print Layout' option returns you to the normal screen.

## A2.7 Finding and replacing text in your document

If you want to find specific words or phrases in your document, to change the spelling (or text formatting, e.g. italics) or to replace them with alternative wording, use '_Home/Find_' ('**Ctrl+F**') or '_Home/Replace_' ('**Ctrl+H**'). Each instance of the chosen text is presented in turn and you are asked whether you want to replace it. Alternatively you can automatically replace all instances.

## A2.8 Saving your work regularly and keeping back-ups

Get into the habit of saving your work regularly as you word-process (every 10 minutes or so) so if the computer 'goes down' or crashes, your work will not all be lost. You can set up _Word_ to save your work automatically, for example, every 10 minutes, using '_Office Button/Word Options/Save_' and then select the '_Save Autorecover information every_' box, while inserting an appropriate time interval in the box available. This will mean that if the system crashes there is a reasonable chance that _Word_ will be able to recover most of what you've done. Another important tip to remember is to keep at least one back-up of your work on a mobile storage device such as a CD-ROM, DVD or a USB key in case anything bad happens to your computer, usually the night before an assignment is due to be handed in!

> **Note**
>
> If you want to send your document to others who have the previous version of _Microsoft Office_, remember to save it in a form compatible with that version by choosing 'Word 97-2003 Document' in the 'Save as type' window.

## A2.9 Don't be afraid to explore!

By exploring the functions of _Word_ for yourself, you will soon become more familiar with the toolbar and menu options. If you get an unexpected result, '**Ctrl+Z**' will take you back to your previous stage. You can also add the 'Undo' icon to the 'Quick Access' toolbar (see _Section A1.1_). With practice and using the 'Help' facility (described below) you can explore the features and extend your knowledge.

## A2.9.1 Using the Help facility in Word

_Word_ provides a useful 'Help' facility that you can view through the help icon at the top right hand of the screen (shown in Figure A3), or by pressing '**F1**', which can quickly explain how to do things. You are presented with a menu that gives information about a variety of topics. If you are unable to find the answer to your problem there, you can try typing a keyword or phrase into the 'Search' box, shown in Figure A4. Alternatively,

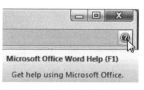

Microsoft Office Word Help (F1)

Get help using Microsoft Office.

you could try doing a

**Figure A3 The Help button**

**Figure A4 The Search box**

search on the internet – it is very likely that others will have encountered a similar problem to you and have posted up advice on how to deal with it.

# A3 Producing polished documents: formatting tips

There are three principal types of formatting: character formatting, paragraph formatting and page formatting. *Word* mainly handles the first two of these through the 'Home' ribbon and page formatting (described in *Section A3.5*) through the 'Page Layout' ribbon, although this also covers aspects of paragraph formatting. The following tips cover formatting characters first and formatting pages last, but you may find it preferable to set the page format before embarking on your work.

## A3.1 Character formatting

The 'Font' group of the 'Home' ribbon (Figure A5) contains a variety of icons representing commonly used options such as the font type (e.g. Arial, Times New Roman, Comic Sans MS), size (*e.g.* 8 point, 12 point and 18 point) and style (including **bold**, *italics* and underlined). You can produce subscripts and superscripts by selecting your text and clicking on the appropriate icon; these are useful for molecular formulae such as $H_3O^+$. Remember, however, that superscripts and subscripts can be produced more quickly with shortcut key combinations, as explained earlier. Further possibilities can be obtained via the 'Font' dialogue box (shown in Figure A6), which appears when you click on the

**Figure A5 The Font group**

**Figure A6 The Font Formatting dialogue box**

arrow at the bottom right-hand side of the 'Font' group or via '*Home/Font*'. A variety of character spacing effects may also be obtained through the relevant options in this dialogue box. Different permutations of all these can be included in the same piece of text, by selecting different parts and then reformatting. Remember to confirm your choices each time by clicking on the 'OK' button at the bottom.

### A3.1.1 Non-breaking spaces and hyphens

To prevent numbers becoming separated from their units, as might occur if the page formatting positions them at the end of a line (e.g. 362 nmol $l^{-1}$), you can insert '*non-breaking*' *spaces* ('**Ctrl+Shift+spacebar**'). These appear as small circles (362°nmol°$l^{-1}$) when the 'Show/Hide' icon ¶ in the 'Paragraph' group of the 'Home' ribbon is selected (also activated by '**Ctrl+Shift+***'). Similarly, to prevent hyphenated words from becoming split into two parts '*non-breaking*' *hyphens* ('**Ctrl+Shift+hyphen**') can be employed.

## A3.2 Paragraph formatting

Paragraphs are recognized by *Word* as pieces of text separated by a carriage return (inserted with the '**Return**' or '**Enter**' key). All the carriage returns will show on the screen by selecting the 'Show/Hide' icon ¶ in the 'Home' ribbon (or '**Ctrl+Shift+***'). This also makes the character spacing visible and can be useful when checking the formatting of the document.

The 'Paragraph' dialogue box, shown in Figure A7, is very useful for formatting paragraphs. It can be seen if you position the cursor within the paragraph that you want to change, then either select '*Home/Paragraph*' or right-click the mouse and select '*Paragraph*' from the shortcut menu that appears.

**Figure A7 The Paragraph formatting dialogue box**

### A3.2.1 Line spacing

Spacing between lines can be adjusted via the 'Line Spacing' icon in the 'Home' ribbon or by selecting '*Line Spacing*' in the 'Paragraph' dialogue box and then choosing one of the options presented, *e.g.* 'Single', '1.5 lines', 'Double'. This paragraph is in double line spacing.

If you have an essay that just goes into an extra page with your preferred spacing then you could choose your own intermediate spacing using the 'Multiple' option, e.g. 1.3 spacing, as in this paragraph.

## A3.2.2 Spacing before and after a paragraph

To ensure that your paragraphs are clearly separated, it is a good idea to specify a '*Spacing Before*' or a '*Spacing After*' setting in the 'Paragraph' dialogue box. If a paragraph has a 'space before' setting of '6 pt', this gives a gap of half a line where the text is in 12 point size and it enables the paragraph gap to be seen clearly, without taking up as much space as an entire blank line. Except when dealing with the special case of headings (see *Section A3.3*), it is best to achieve your paragraph gaps by setting only one of the spacings and stick to that. If you mix the two, then you're likely to get inconsistencies when different styles of paragraphs are put together.

## A3.2.3 Alignment of the text

Paragraphs can be aligned to the left, to the right, to both right and left (also called justified) or centred by selecting the appropriate alignment options in the '*Paragraph*' group of the 'Home' ribbon. These alignments are illustrated in Table A2, together with the appropriate icons and the shortcut key combinations.

**Table A2 Different ways of justifying text**

| This paragraph is aligned to the left margin. This setting is good for letters, as it gives documents a less 'word-processed' feel. | This paragraph is aligned to the right margin. This setting is commonly used for addresses on letters, and can also be useful to allow space for diagrams, etc. | This paragraph is justified. *Word* automatically widens the gaps between words so the text is flush with both the left and right margins. | This paragraph is centred. This setting is useful for titles and headings, or for diagrams, etc. |
|---|---|---|---|
| ('Ctrl+L') | ('Ctrl+R') | ('Ctrl+J') | ('Ctrl+E') |

**Paragraph settings for essays.** For essays, an advisable format is 11 point Arial font, left-aligned, with *at least* 1.5 line spacing to give room for markers to write comments between the lines, although you might find that some tutors prefer double spacing. Also, remember to set a suitable margin size, through the 'Page Setup' dialogue box, obtained by clicking the arrow at the bottom right-hand side of the 'Page Setup' group in the 'Page Layout' ribbon. Essays should always have margins of at least a couple of centimetres or so for comments, but again the precise settings can be tweaked to fit pages better.

**Tabs.** Tab stop positions are fixed horizontal measurements across the text that can be used to ensure that appropriate parts of different lines align correctly, for example in the following little table, which shows the indents of the first four standard tab stop positions in inches and centimetres[6].

| tab 1 | tab 2 | tab 3 | tab 4 |
|-------|-------|-------|-------|
| 0.5   | 1     | 1.5   | 2     |
| 1.27  | 2.54  | 3.81  | 5.08  |

Pressing the '**Tab**' key normally takes the cursor up to the next tab stop position, with subsequent text continuing at that point (this is called a 'Left' tab), but you can also define other types of tab position, to produce effects like these (the first line of letters shows where the tab positions are):

| C | R | L | D | L | R |
|---|---|---|---|---|---|
| This shows | This shows | *A 'Decimal'* | 123 | *A 'Right' tab* .........1 | |
| the | the | *tab does this:* | 365.26 | *with a 'Leader':* ....2 | |
| effect of a | effect of a | | 3.1416 | ------------------------3 | |
| 'Centre' tab | 'Right' tab | | .01 | _____4 | |

You can set the tab stop positions, and their types, through '*Home/Paragraph/Tab*' or '*Page Layout/Paragraph/Tabs*' (which make the same dialogue box visible). This enables you to set the 'default' tab spacing for any paragraphs you've selected, and to set or clear any other tabs. If you want to have a line leading up to the tab (a 'Leader') you can choose from four styles in the 'Tab' formatting box.

**Rulers.** To help you organize your tab stop positions (and also the vertical positioning of your document), you can create 'rulers' along the top and down the left-hand side of your document using '*View/Ruler*'. (The little icon at the top of the vertical scroll bar can also be clicked to make the rulers appear or disappear). The top ruler shows the position of the left margin, any indents, and also tab stops that apply to all your selected text. Figure A8, for example, shows the left-hand part of the ruler that appears if the cursor is placed in one of the specially tabbed lines in the previous paragraph (note that the different types of tab are indicated by different symbols). If you position the cursor over a tab symbol on the ruler, it changes into a double-headed arrow, a dotted vertical line appears, extending downwards from the tab, and you can then drag the tab to a different position along the ruler.

**Figure A8  Different tabs on the ruler**

---

6  You can fix whether *Word* uses inches or centimetres through '*Office Button/Word Options*' and then going to 'Display' in the 'Advanced' menu.

---

**Tip**

To ensure a consistent layout for your documents, it is far better to set general tab positions using the dialogue box, where the measurements can be specified precisely rather than 'guessing' using the ruler. The ruler is particularly useful to set tab stop positions in special cases; for example, where you have some particular odd paragraph to sort out. The ruler can also be very useful as a guide when positioning objects in the document as described in *Section A3.6.2*.

---

### Indents

**Whole paragraph indents** are useful where parts of the text need to stand out from the main body. This paragraph has an indentation of 1 cm from the left-and right-hand sides of the page; such indenting from both margins is most commonly used for 'block quotations'. The 'Paragraph' group of the 'Home' ribbon provides shortcut icons ( ▤ and ▤ ) for increasing and decreasing respectively the left indents by the size of the current default 'tab' setting. If you want any other indentation you will need to use either the 'Paragraph' dialogue box (through '*Home/Paragraph/Tabs*' or '*Page Layout/Paragraph/Tabs*') or, alternatively, drag the indent marker to a different position on the horizontal ruler.

**First line indents,** as illustrated here, can be used to show clearly where a paragraph begins, which is particularly useful where there is no spacing between paragraphs. This effect can be obtained through the 'Paragraph' dialogue box and then '*Special*' and '*First line*' (see *Figure A9*).

The advantage of producing first line indents in this way, rather than by using the '**Tab**' key, is that it makes it easier to

**Figure A9  Setting paragraph indentation**

ensure a consistent layout and to change your paragraph formatting if you wish to do so. This point is particularly important if you take advantage of *Word*'s facilities for style definition, explained in *Section A3.3*.

### Hanging indents

(a) A hanging indent applies to every line of the paragraph *except the first*. Its main use is to produce numbered or itemized lists, as illustrated here, and this effect is obtained through '*Special*' followed by '*Hanging*' in the 'Paragraph' dialogue box. After the initial '(a)', '1.' or whatever, press '**Tab**' to reach the appropriate position for the rest of the first line.

(b) It is a very bad idea to try to produce this effect 'by hand' using the '**Tab**' key on each line after the first, because if you do, any change to the text or the margins is likely to produce an awful mess with tab characters in the middle of lines.

> **Tip**
>
> Remember to use hanging indents for the effect shown in the previous two paragraphs. Do not use the '**Tab**' key except in the very first line of a paragraph.

### Bullets and numbering

Information can be clearly grouped using bullets and numbering systems. Various styles are available in the 'Paragraph' group of the 'Home' ribbon via the down arrows next to the bullet ⋮≡ ▾ or numbering ⌁≡ ▾ icons, and there is also a multilevel option. For example:

- bullets
  - ➤ symbols (count as 'bulleted')
    1. numbers
       a) letters (count as 'numbered')

Using 'Bullets' or 'Numbering' will automatically create hanging indents as described above.

## A3.2.4  Borders and shading

> Borders and Shading can be applied to all or part of a selected paragraph via '**Alt+H/Alt+B**' and '**Alt+H/Alt+H**' or by using the 'Borders' and the 'Shading' ♦▾ ⊞ ▾ icons in the 'Home' ribbon. This paragraph has borders (select 'Outside Borders') and is shaded with 'White Background 1, Darker 15%'.

## A3.3  Saving time by setting your styles

When you are producing documents such as projects and reports you can waste time simply

**Figure A10  The Styles gallery**

by selecting different font styles and spacings between the main text, a heading and a sub-heading. *Word* has a particularly useful facility that minimizes the time spent on this, by allowing you to store pre-defined settings for a heading, sub-heading, etc. This facility is available via the 'Styles' group in the 'Home' ribbon. *Word* displays several pre-defined headings in the 'Quick Styles Gallery', such as 'Normal' (representing the format of the main text), 'Heading' 1', Heading 2', etc., as shown in Figure A10. The scroll bar at the right of the gallery allows you to see the whole contents. You can assess the effect of each of these types of formatting, quickly, by positioning your cursor over each style and watching how your text changes. Since the 'Heading' styles are defined to include the text in the following paragraph (usually termed 'Normal'), every time you want to use this set-up, you can simply click on the appropriate style and start typing; having typed your heading, and pressed the **'Return'** key the font will automatically change to whichever style has been chosen to follow. There are many pre-defined styles. These can be viewed in the 'Styles' window that appears after clicking on the arrow in the bottom right hand of the 'Styles' group[7]. You can see the features of a style by

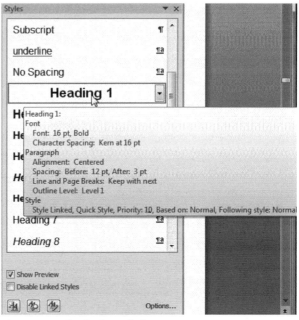

**Figure A11 The Styles window**

pointing the cursor at its name. For example, Heading 1 in Figure A11 has been pre-defined to be centred in 16 pt Arial bold, with a 12 pt gap before and a 3 pt gap to follow. Any styles that you use regularly are worth adding to your 'Quick Styles Gallery'. Do this by positioning the mouse over the style you need, click on the down-arrow that appears on the right and select '*Add to Quick Style Gallery*'. Styles you don't need can be removed from this gallery by right-clicking over them and selecting '*Remove from Quick Style Gallery*'.

## A3.3.1 Defining your own styles

You do not always have to use these pre-defined styles but can modify an existing style and also create a new style. To modify an existing style, position the mouse over its name in the 'Styles' window, click on the down-arrow that appears on the right of the name and select '*Modify*'. Through the 'Modify Style' dialogue box that appears, you can make various changes either directly or via '*Format*' at the bottom of the box. To create a new style, click on the 'New Style' icon ![icon] at the bottom of the 'Styles' window. A 'Create New Style from Formatting' dialogue box appears, shown in Figure A12; you should choose a suitable name for your style and fix the following three settings:

• '*Style type*'('Paragraph' is the usual choice);

---

7  If you find that the Styles Window is cluttered with huge numbers of format descriptions, remove the tick from the '*Office Button/Word Options/Advanced/Editing options/Keep track of formatting*' checkbox. If this is ticked, then *Word* automatically displays a style to correspond to the editing you do, whether you are planning to reuse the style or not.

- '*Style based on*' (e.g. 'Heading 1' – choose the existing style that is closest to the one you want to define, so you do not have to specify too many distinctive features);

- '*Style for following paragraph*' ('Normal' would be the usual choice, unless you want your header to be followed by some other specific style of paragraph, such as for the first paragraph of a new section).

Then click on '*Format*' to define the various features of your style in the same way you would format a paragraph of text. Having done this, click on 'OK' and the name you chose for the style will appear in the 'Quick Styles Gallery'. You can check how you've defined it at any time by pointing the cursor at it in the 'Styles' window. If you later want to modify or delete the style, you can do so using the down-arrow. Remember, however, that this will change each instance of that style throughout the entire document with which you are working.

**Figure A12 The Create New Style dialogue box**

It is a good idea to create a quick access link to your 'Quick Style Gallery' through the 'Quick Access Toolbar' by right-clicking over any part of the gallery and selecting '*Add Gallery to Quick Access Toolbar*' from the menu, as illustrated in Figure A13.

**Figure A13 Quick access to Styles**

## A3.3.2 Planning styles for your essays

If you plan your styles carefully, they can be used for many different documents and you can save huge amounts of time. For example, you might set the styles for all your essays to include:

'*Normal*': 11 point, Arial, left-aligned, no indents, with a few Left tab positions (e.g. 1.27 cm, 2.54 cm, 3.81 cm), and a Right tab position to coincide with the right-hand page margin (e.g. at 16 cm for A4 paper with a 2.5 cm margin all round).

'*FirstLine*': based on '*Normal*', but with a first line indent of 1.27 cm.

'*Hanging 1*': based on '*Normal*', but with a single hanging indent (e.g. 1.27 cm).

'*Hanging 2*': based on '*Normal*', but indented 2.54 cm from the left.

'*BlockIndent*': based on '*Normal*', but indented 1.27 cm from both left and right, single-spaced, and 10 point type.

'*Headings*': use the *Word* 'Heading' styles, editing these to your taste (for example, by centring them). Do not define completely new styles for headers, because using the *Word* 'Heading' styles enables you to use the document Map and Outline View facilities (described in *Section A2.6*) and also to produce tables of contents automatically (described in *Section A3.4*).

### A3.3.3  Using your styles for other documents

Having defined your styles in the manner that you want (and saved your document), delete any text in the document and save it as a template using '*Office Button/ Save As*' and then choosing '*Word Template*' in the '*Save as type*' drop-down menu. Give the template a suitable name (e.g. 'Essay'), and you will be able to incorporate it within any new essay file by selecting it (from 'New from existing' or 'My templates' in the 'Templates' task pane) whenever you create a file using '*Office Button/New*'.

### A3.4  Quick and easy tables of contents, and lists of figures and tables

If you use the 'Styles' facility consistently for the headings and sub-headings throughout your work, an added bonus is that you can then easily generate a table of contents for your document. To do this, first position the cursor at the point where you want the table to appear in your document. For a table of contents with just three heading levels you can simply click on '*Table of Contents*' in the '*References*' ribbon ('**Alt+S/Alt+T**') and pick one of the automatic styles. You will find that a nicely formatted table is produced for you automatically, with all the correct page numbers. Moreover, if you later change the document by adding or removing pages, you can easily create a revised table of

**Figure A14  The Index and Tables Formatting dialogue box**

contents by right-clicking on the existing table and selecting '*Update Field*' from the shortcut menu. Other styles can be obtained using the '*Insert Table of Contents*' option at the bottom of the 'Table of Contents' menu (alternatively via '*References/Table of Contents/Insert Table of Contents*'). In the dialogue box that appears (shown in Figure A14) you can choose various modifications, and once you are satisfied with the result, click on 'OK'.

*Word* can also link figures and tables to the number of the page on which they appear, which allows you to create an index of figures or tables. To enable *Word* to identify when you are inserting a numbered figure and its title or caption, you must press '*References/Insert Caption*' and then add your caption to your figure in the box provided, as shown in Figure A15. Once you have included all the figures and their accompanying captions, you can go to the 'Table of Figures' dialogue box (via '*References/Insert Table of Figures*') and click on 'OK'.

**Figure A15  The Caption dialogue box**

## A3.4.1  Inserting cross-references

The cross-references facility, available through '*References*'/*Cross-reference*' (in the 'Captions' group) or via '*Insert/Cross-reference*', keeps track of elements such as footnotes, figures and tables, etc. The 'Cross-reference' dialogue box is shown in Figure A16. If you use this to insert cross-references and then reformat the document or later change the numbering of these elements (by insertions or deletions, etc.), then *Word* will automatically adjust the cross-references appropriately to retain the correct link. So, for example, you can say 'see footnote 3' or 'refer to the figure on page 5' without having to worry about re-checking the references if the numbering of the footnotes or the pagination of the figures changes. Remember to revise these using '*Update Field*' from the shortcut menu for your finished document.

**Figure A16  The Cross-reference dialogue box**

## A3.5  Page formatting

The overall appearance of the document can be adjusted very quickly via facilities in the 'Page Setup' group of the 'Page Layout' ribbon. This provides a range of pre-set margins, and offers a choice of orientation (portrait or landscape) and size. For non-standard settings you must go to the 'Page Setup' dialogue box, illustrated in Figure A17, activated by clicking on the arrow in the bottom right of the 'Page setup' group (or via **'Alt+P/Alt+S+P'**). In addition, the options available in the 'Layout' tab within this box allow you to adjust the margins for the headers and footers where you insert such things as page numbers and chapter headings.

**Figure A17  The Page Setup dialogue box**

When doing this sort of editing, you will need to be able to see how the document looks on the page, so you should select '*View/Print Layout*' if you have not already done so.

Adding headers, footers and page numbers to your document can make it look more polished; they can help orientate the reader and, if you include the date the document was produced, they are useful for identifying specific versions of documents quickly. By double-clicking over the footer region on any page you can view the Headers and Footers, which can then be edited. '*Insert/Header*' or '*Insert/Footer*' can be used as alternative routes. Double-clicking over the main body of the text returns you to the print layout view.

### A3.5.1 Inserting section and page breaks

If you want different sections of the document to have different formatting (layout, orientation, header, etc.), use '*Page Layout/Breaks*' (in the 'Page Setup' group) to divide it into sections. If you deselect the '*Same as Previous*' option in the header/footer toolbar, you can apply different headers and footers to the different sections. '*Insert/Break*' simply inserts a break so that a new page follows on from that position.

## A3.6 Inserting and formatting objects in your document

### A3.6.1 Inserting pictures, diagrams and objects

The 'Insert' ribbon allows you to insert a variety of items into your document. Illustrations can be inserted through '*Insert/Picture*', '*Insert/Shapes*', '*Insert/ SmartArt*', '*Insert/Chart*'. Inserting Clip Art requires **'Alt+N/Alt+F'**. You can also insert objects and text boxes using '*Insert*' followed by the relevant selection ('*Object*' or '*Text Box*').

Pictures of a screen shot (everything that appears on your monitor screen) can be copied into the Clipboard (described in *Section A2.4*) using the **'Print Screen'** key ('**PrtScr**') and then pasted into your document via **'Ctrl V'** or '*Paste*' in the 'Clipboard' group of the 'Home' ribbon. If you hold the **'Alt'** key down at the same time, then only the currently active window will be copied.

**Figure A18  The Format ribbon**

You can change the appearance of inserted pictures or objects through the facilities in the 'Format' ribbon, illustrated in Figure A18, which becomes visible when you select the illustration or object (by clicking over it once, or using the selection tool – details about this can be found in *Section A5.3*). Standard options available in the 'Format' ribbon include the ability to change an object's colour, appearance, arrangement on the page, and size. The quickest way to resize an object, however, is to click on it. This makes the edges of the object visible with dark-coloured 'resize' boxes and circles spaced along the sides and at the corners. Positioning the cursor over a resize box changes it into a double-headed arrow ⇦⇨ (a 'resize' handle) with which you can drag (with the left mouse button depressed) the margins to a more appropriate position. If you resize at a corner you can avoid distortion of the object.

> **Note**
>
> The options that you are offered in the 'Format' ribbon will vary according to the type of object that you are formatting. For example, different style effects are available for pictures and text boxes, and a 'Text' group is included in the 'Format' ribbon for the text boxes but not for pictures.

### A3.6.2 Positioning the object on the page

If you find that your inserted object is difficult to position on the page or it 'jumps' around when you add more text or other objects, you will need to adjust the 'Text Wrapping' settings in the 'Arrange' group of the 'Format' ribbon (Figure A19). The 'Text Wrapping' facility is also available in the 'Page Layout' ribbon. Selecting the '*Tight*' and '*Square*' settings allows you to drag the image to an appropriate place on your page with the text flowing around it, whereas the '*In line with text*' setting excludes text from the horizontal space next to it. If you still have trouble placing your object on the page the 'More Layout Options…' button at the bottom of the 'Text Wrapping' menu can be useful – it takes you to an 'Advanced Layout' dialogue box within which you can adjust the object's position manually. You can also use the 'Position' facility in the 'Arrange' group for positioning the object on the page.

**Figure A19  The Text Wrapping settings**

### A3.6.3  Keeping the file size of images small

Some images that you may wish to insert into your work require very large amounts of storage space, particularly those produced in *Microsoft Paint* or *Paintbrush* (these are 'bitmaps' and have the file extension '.bmp'), scanned pictures, photographs, and images copied from the internet (with file extensions such as .tif and .png)[8]. When several of these are inserted into a document, the file can take a long time to open and could cause problems if you try to email it to others.

**Figure A20  Saving pictures**

You can attempt to overcome this by reducing the size of images **before** inserting them into a document. First, save the image by right-clicking over the image to activate the sub-menu (like the one shown in Figure A20) and then choose '*Save Picture As/Save as type*'. You may be given the option of saving a bitmap image as a 'jpg' file (for '*Joint Photographics Expert Group file*' or '*JPEG*') which may result in a slight loss of resolution, but which will reduce the size of the file as you save it.

If you are not given this option in the menu, or you wish to obtain even more compression, save the image with its original file extension (e.g. .bmp, .tif or .png), and then open it in a graphics package such as *Paint Shop Pro*. You can then save it with a different ('compressing') file extension, such as 'jpg' and 'gif'. If you choose a 'gif' extension

**Figure A21  Saving a picture with a different file extension**

---

8  If you copy an image from the internet by right-clicking over the picture, selecting *Copy*, and then pasting it into your document *Word* may automatically compress the picture slightly, with some loss of resolution.

('*Graphics Interchange Format*' file or 'GIF'), as shown in Figure A21, your image will be limited to 256 colours. This drawback, however, is unlikely to be a problem for the types of diagrams and illustrations you might use in scientific reports, and is far outweighed by the increased efficiency of file storage.

The 'JPEG' format is good for photographs, but poor for line drawings, graphs and other diagrams since it makes lines fuzzy, as illustrated in Figure A22. The 'GIF' format is a good way to store line drawings, graphs, etc. since it preserves the sharpness of lines.

An alternative (but not always successful) way of compressing documents containing large images is via '*Compress Pictures*' in the 'Adjust' group of the 'Format' ribbon.

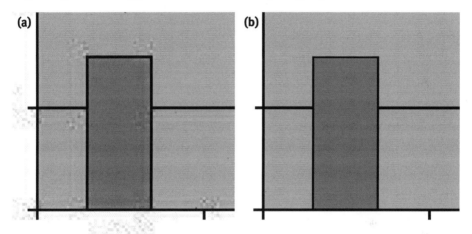

**Figure A22  Close-up of part a graph saved in (a) JPEG format and (b) GIF format**

## A3.6.4  Inserting text boxes

Putting text into text boxes is a useful way of creating a section of a document that can be positioned independently of the rest, or highlighted. Having created the box ('*Insert/Text Box*') and typed in some text you can then treat the box as an independent entity as shown in the vertical text on the right here. More information about text boxes is included in *Section A5.1*.

The main drawback of using text boxes is that if you decide to change the font style (for example, from one that is fairly compact, such as Times New Roman to one that is less compact, such as Arial), or size, the box may not expand downwards to accommodate all of the text so you may lose the final part if it expands beyond the box size.

A particularly useful facility for science students and those who present data in the form of graphs, is the ability to format text boxes so their text runs vertically up or down, as might be used for legends to a *y*-axis. Having selected the text box, the 'Format' ribbon will appear. Successive clicks on '*Text Direction*' within the 'Text' group of the ribbon will rotate the text. You can remove the borders of the text box via '*Shape Outline*' ('*No outline*' option) in the '*Text Box Styles*' group of the ribbon.

### A3.6.5 Formatting text around the insert

Allowing the text to flow round an inserted object can give a more interesting and polished look to your document. This is achieved through *'Format/Text Wrapping'*, and subsequently selecting from the various options (*'In line with text'*, *'Square'*, *'Tight'*, etc.) as described in

( This object has a 'tight' wrapping. )

Section A3.6.2. Pick one that suits the look of the text. Remember that the *'More Layout Options'* button at the bottom of the 'Text Wrapping' menu can be useful to help you place your object on the page.

### A3.6.6 Inserting unusual symbols

Scientific notation often involves the use of symbols ($\alpha$, $\beta$, $\mu$, $\div$, $\geq$, $\pm$, etc.). These are obtained through the 'Symbols' group of the 'Insert' ribbon (**'Alt+N/Alt+U'**). The initial list displayed may not contain the symbol you want. If so, select *'More Symbols'* to view the 'Symbol' dialogue box, in which there are many more options (see Figure A23). Symbols and functions for mathematical equations can also be inserted using the 'Equation' option.

**Figure A23  The Symbol dialogue box**

### A3.7 Using tables for clear presentation

Scientific data can often be presented more tidily in tables rather than as lists. To insert a table, select *'Insert/Table'* (as shown in Figure A24) and drag the cursor over the grid to get the required number of rows and columns. For larger tables, you must activate the 'Insert Table' dialogue box (using *'Insert Table'* in the menu) and type in the appropriate numbers manually. Note that two more tabs, 'Design' and 'Layout', appear in the tabbed menu when you are working on a table.

A quick way of changing the number of columns and rows from an existing table is by positioning the cursor above a column or alongside a row until it turns into a 'selection' arrow, as shown in Figure A25, then right-clicking on the mouse and selecting the relevant insert or delete command from the shortcut menu shown in Figure A26. Alternatively, use

**Figure A24  Inserting tables**

**Figure A25 Column selection**

the 'Rows & Columns' group from the 'Layout' ribbon ('**Alt+J+L**'). From this you can '*Insert Above*' ('*Below*' / '*Left*' / '*Right*') and also '*Delete*'. You can quickly change the size of cells by positioning the cursor over the line to be moved. The cursor will change into a resize line symbol +‖+, and you can then drag the line to the position you want. Alternatively you can select the part you want

to change (by dragging the mouse over the relevant cells with the left-hand button depressed), right-click the mouse and select '*Table Properties*' from the shortcut menu (shown in Figure A26). This contains many of the formatting options in the 'Layout' ribbon and is often quicker to use.

You may be able to improve the presentation of a table by changing the borders and the shading of the cells. Various options are available through the 'Borders and Shading' dialogue box shown in Figure A27, obtained from the shortcut menu. This dialogue box can also be reached from the 'Borders' option in the 'Design' ribbon. By default, *Word* gives a border to each cell. While this may be useful when creating your table, it can give a cluttered appearance in the final document.

**Figure A26 The Table Formatting menu**

If you want to present data as a list rather than in a boxed table, then you can still use a *Word* table structure but remove the borders. To do this, choose '*No Border*' from '*Borders*', or '*None*' from the 'Borders and Shading' dialogue box. Other design options are available in the 'Table Styles' group of the 'Design' ribbon but do be careful to keep the style appropriate to your work. One advantage of putting data

into a tabular form is that you avoid the use of repeated '**Tab**' characters, which keeps formatting much simpler and also makes it more likely that you will retain a tidy appearance if slight changes are made to any of the data. Another advantage is that if you decide to increase the size of the font within the cell, the cell will expand downwards to accommodate it.

**Figure A27 The Borders and Shading dialogue box**

| | | | |
|---|---|---|---|
| Text may be positioned in different parts of a cell. Right-click the mouse when the cursor is over the cell to be formatted, then choose '*Cell Alignment*' | In this cell the text is aligned in the bottom right-hand corner… | The horizontal borders have been removed from the cells in this column (using '*Borders*' in the 'Design' ribbon). | This cell has text aligned at the top. |
| Individual cells can be shaded via '*Shading*' in the 'Design' ribbon | …whereas in this one, it is aligned in the top left. | | Cells can / also be / split into / sub-cells |
| Several cells may be merged (select cells, right-click the mouse then choose '*Merge Cells*'). This is useful for table titles and legends. | | | |

### A3.7.1  Bulk operations on an entire table

To save time you can perform operations on entire tables rather than repeating the same operation on each cell. Clicking on any part of the table will make a small cross appear at the top left-hand corner of the table as shown in Figure A28. Clicking on this cross will select the entire table and you can then choose the formatting commands as appropriate.

**Figure A28 Whole table selection**

### A3.7.2  Changing plain text and lists into a table (or vice versa)

You can convert your text into a table using '*Insert/Table/Convert Text To Table*'. Words separated by '**Tab**' characters in your plain text will appear in consecutive cells. You can also convert tables to text; (via the 'Data' group in the 'Layout' ribbon) here you get a choice of items used to separate the contents of cells in the original table including paragraph marks, tabs, commas, and other options that you can define yourself.

### A3.8  Multi-column documents

Documents with several columns can be produced using '*Columns*' ('**Alt+J**') in the '*P*age Layout' ribbon. Different column layouts can be chosen for different sections – for example, this little section was selected to have three columns (two columns of text and one column for the figure), as illustrated in Figure A29. The text automatically continues into a new column unless you insert a column break (using '*Page Layout/Break/ Column*' or by pressing '**Ctrl+Shift+Return**').

**Figure A29 Creating columns**

## A3.9  Spelling, grammar, thesaurus and word count

Spelling and grammar in a whole document or selected portions of text can be checked using '*Review/Spelling and Grammar*' or '**F7**'. *Word* can be set up to highlight incorrect spelling and grammar, via '*Office Button/Word Options/Proofing*'. Make sure, however, that *Word* is set up for British rather than American English (through '*Office Button/Word Options/Popular/Language Settings*'), and be aware that the spell checker cannot distinguish between homonyms such as 'there' and 'their', or 'sea' and 'see', so it is important to proof-read your documents carefully. You can add words to *Word*'s dictionary (but check that your spelling is correct before doing so), which can be useful when dealing with scientific nomenclature and technical terminology. The grammar checker can be rather fussy and doesn't always get things right (so don't rely entirely on it), but can be useful to pick up some of the more obvious slips.

The thesaurus facility is very useful when trying to think of words with similar meaning to avoid repetition or remind yourself of a word you've forgotten. Type a word close in meaning to the one you want, then select '*Review/Thesaurus*' or press '**Shift+F7**'.

If you are limited to a certain number of words for an essay, *Word* helpfully displays the word count in the status bar at the bottom of the screen. The word count of selected portions (e.g. a paragraph), can also be displayed, including those in text boxes. Hyphenated words count only once.

## A3.10 Printing your document

### A3.10.1 Check the layout

Always check the layout on the printed page before printing using '*Office Button/ 'Print/Print Preview*', ('**Alt+F/Alt+W/Alt+V**'), or '**Ctrl+F2**'. This should be done *after* you have specified which printer is to be used; otherwise you might be surprised by the finished printed document; different printer characteristics, e.g. dots per inch, can result in different formatting. If you find that changes must be made, this will save you time, and will be much cheaper on ink and paper, or printer credits.

### A3.10.2 Setting your printer

When you come to print, bear in mind that many printers now allow options such as double-sided printing, and most will allow you to put two (or even four) pages of your document on a sheet. To do this, select '*Office Button/Print*' ('**Alt+F/Alt+P**') then click on the '*Properties*' button, as shown in Figure A30. This may take you straight to the appropriate dialogue box for choosing your options. You may, however, need to look for further options (such as '*Finishing*' pictured in Figure A31) before you can

**Figure A30  Printer options**

set the print layout. If your vision is good, two pages per sheet should be fine to read, but do not submit essays in that form!

**Figure A31 Setting the printing layout**

# A4 Using the Review ribbon

It is worth getting to know the functions accessed by the 'Review' ribbon, since they can streamline the whole process of producing a finished document. This ribbon gives access to facilities that allow you to compare early and later versions of your work, to assist with group collaboration, and also enables you to receive electronic feedback from others.

## A4.1 *Keeping track of changes to your document*

When you create word-processed documents, you may end up producing several different saved versions, and this brings with it the danger that you could forget which is the best, especially if you work on your document in different places, saving the various versions on more than one computer (for instance on the university network and also on your home computer). The *'Compare'* facility in the 'Review' ribbon can help reduce this risk, allowing you to compare documents, to identify the sections that have been changed and to retain those that are more appropriate.

To compare documents, open one version and then choose *'Review/Compare/ Compare'*. This opens a 'Compare Documents' dialogue box (shown in Figure A32) inviting you to browse on the computer for the files you want for comparison. Having confirmed your choice by clicking 'OK' a new window will appear containing four

**Figure A32 The Compare Documents dialogue box**

smaller windows[9] illustrated in Figure A33. The left-hand 'Reviewing Pane' displays all the revisions made in the document, the centre window contains your file with the differences highlighted, while the two smaller windows on the right show the original and revised files, respectively. Double-clicking on a revision takes you directly to that place in your document. When you right-click over a revision you are presented with a sub-menu which allows you to accept or reject it. If you decide you want to accept or reject all the changes in a selected part of the document simultaneously, a quick way to do this is via '*Review/ Accept / Accept All Changes in document*'.

**Figure A33  The Comparing Documents display**

If you prefer, you can set any revisions to be shown within 'balloons' in the margin next to the change as in Figure A34 so that they look something like those shown in Figure A35.

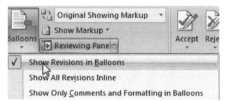

**Figure A34  Selecting for revisions in balloons**

If you are unsure which version of your document you prefer, you can switch between the original and revised file in the 'Compare Document' window by clicking on the 'Final Showing Markup' down-arrow in the 'Tracking' group of the 'Review' ribbon and choose '*Original Showing Markup*' as shown in Figure A36.

**Figure A36  Different Markup views**

**Figure A35  Showing revisions in balloons**

---

9  This layout can be altered using '*Review/Show Source documents*' and '*Review/Reviewing Pane*' or '**Alt+T+P**'.

> **Note**
>
> You can print any one of the four versions of your document by selecting the appropriate option from the 'Tracking' group. You may also find that the 'Print' dialogue box gives you the option of printing the document with or without its markup.

## A4.2 Producing a document through group collaboration and receiving electronic feedback from supervisors

If you are working on a document in collaboration with others, the 'Track Changes' facility from the 'Review' ribbon is particularly useful and can quickly be reached via **'Ctrl+Shift+E'**. It works in a similar way to the '*Compare*' function in that any changes made to a document are highlighted, and a note made of the original content. These changes can be placed within the text or as 'balloons' in the margin alongside the change. Again, these revisions can be accepted or rejected by placing the cursor over the change, right-clicking the mouse and selecting from the shortcut menu. If several people contribute to the document, each person will be allocated a different colour[10], so a record is retained of which changes were made and by whom.

**The Review ribbon¶**

It is worth getting to know the functions accessed by the 'Review' ribbon, because it can streamline the whole process of producing a finished document. This allows you to compare early and later versions of your work, to assist group collaboration over a piece of work and also enables you to receive electronic feedback from others¶

Comment [PEM1]: Add the section number.¶

Comment [PEM2]: Include illustrative diagrams in this section.¶

**Figure A37  Inserting comments**

Usefully, *Word* includes a facility that allows you to add 'comments' to the document. This would be the electronic equivalent of writing notes in the margin of a hard copy; a tool that some supervisors use to give feedback on electronic versions of essays and dissertations. A 'Comments Box' can be inserted alongside any point in the document, as illustrated in Figure A37 (providing you have selected the '*Show revisions in Balloons*' option) by placing the cursor at the point where you wish to make the comment and then using '*Review/New Comment*'. When you have finished making your changes, click once on the 'Track Changes' icon to turn off this facility.

If you receive a document containing changes and comments, you can decide whether to retain or delete the comment by right-clicking over the comment and selecting the appropriate command from the sub-menu that appears.

## A4.3 Ownership and properties of a document

When you create a document its details, such as the name of the author, the date it was created, its size, and its location, are stored in the computer. You can see these properties and make alterations to them through *Windows Explorer* (which can be

---

10  This can be chosen through '*Review/Track Changes* (**'Alt+G'**)*/Change/Tracking Options*'.

conveniently opened at any point by holding down the *Windows* icon key, usually between '**Ctrl**' and '**Alt**' at the bottom left of the keyboard, and typing '**E**'). Right-click on the filename and select '*Properties*' from the shortcut menu.

# A5  Producing drawings in *Word*

If you want to insert a simple diagram, chart or molecular structure into your document that you cannot obtain ready-made, and legitimately, from other sources, *Word* has a drawing facility that is simple to use and surprisingly versatile. Pictures drawn in *Word* generally do not require large amounts of file storage space, which can be an advantage when dealing with large documents. This facility can also insert fancy styles of text commonly known as WordArt. The 'Insert' ribbon contains most of the facilities required to produce basic drawings, but once you start working on a drawing, the 'Format' ribbon (introduced in *Section A3.6.1*) appears, which offers more sophisticated effects.

Other packages such as *Paint* can produce a wider range of drawings in the form of 'raster' or 'bitmap' images (composed of individual dots of colour, like digital photos, rather than geometrical 'vector' patterns), but using *Word* is very convenient; its drawings are likely to appear more precise and less 'grainy' (especially if they are resized), and the stored file is usually much smaller and so takes up less space on the computer hard drive, USB key, etc.

By exploring the various functions in the 'Insert' ribbon you will discover what options are available. Lines, arrows, boxes, circles and more complicated shapes can be drawn after clicking on '*Insert/Shapes*'. Several aspects of these shapes can be altered using the functions in the '*Shape Styles*' group of the 'Format' ribbon. These include the outline style and colour (via '*Shape Outline*') and also the fill-colour of the shapes themselves (via '*Shape Fill*').

## A5.1  Text boxes and the drawing canvas

If you want text to be presented in an unusual way, for instance, for labelling diagrams or to include text running up the side of a vertical axis on a graph, putting it into text boxes may be the best option, as described in *Section A3.6.4*. Text boxes are particularly useful when combined with the 'Grouping' facility, described in *Section A5.3*, for simple reaction equations, because they can retain the appropriate formatting regardless of format changes in the surrounding document.

'*Insert/Text Box*' takes you to a menu from which you can choose a 'custom' text box. You can, however, create your own using the 'Draw Text Box' option at the bottom of this menu. A small text box appears on your screen which is ready for you to type in some text. The box can be repositioned on the page if you make it 'active', by clicking on its border (small dark resize squares will appear along the edges), placing the cursor over one of the edges so that it turns into an 'arrowed' cross ⤯ and then dragging it to another place. You can also quickly resize the box when it is active by placing the cursor over one of the resize squares along the edges, and when it turns into a 'resize' handle, you can drag the edge to a more appropriate position.

Alternatively, right-click over the border of the box and choose '*Format Text Box*' from the shortcut menu. This command takes you to the 'Format Text Box' dialogue box (which can also be activated by clicking on the little arrow at the bottom of the 'Size' group in the 'Format' ribbon). Through this dialogue box you can alter a variety of aspects of the text box, including borders, shading, and the internal margin, as illustrated in Figure

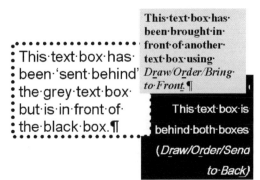

**Figure A38 Formatting text boxes**

A38. This Figure shows that text boxes can also be given the appearance of being positioned in front of, or behind, another object and/or the main text. This is done by right-clicking over the box and then using the '*Order*' sub-menu.

When inserting any drawn object into a file, you have the option to place it inside a drawing

**Figure A39 The drawing canvas**

canvas, shown in Figure A39, created via '*Insert/Shapes/New Drawing Canvas*'. If you do place your drawing within the canvas it will be 'attached' to the canvas and can be moved around within, but not outside it. The advantage of this is that you can insert several objects into the canvas which can then be formatted simultaneously (for instance, copied, deleted, resized or moved). However, using the canvas can restrict your ability to reposition the text box in the document and it is sometimes better to ignore the canvas; you can always move the text box to the correct position later by cutting, pasting, dragging and dropping.

### A5.1.1 Duplicating text boxes

The quickest way to duplicate a text box is to make the box 'active' and then keep the '**Ctrl**' key depressed while dragging a duplicate copy to a new location. The original box will remain in its position. Duplication can also be achieved by making the box active, then right-clicking and selecting '*Copy*' from the shortcut menu. Move the cursor to the new position, right-click and then press '*Paste*' in the sub-menu. Note that placing the cursor inside a text box while pasting anything other than straightforward text into it often gives unpredictable effects and is best avoided, where possible.

### A5.2 Drawing freehand

You can draw objects freehand using '*Insert/Shapes*'. Select the appropriate icon from the '*Lines*' options then click on the part of the screen where you want your drawing to start. For a straight line, release the mouse button and then click a second time at the point you want the line to end. With curves and freehand drawing, you must click *once* every time you want the line to change direction, and double-click at the point you want to finish the line. With the '*Curve*' tool, *Word* automatically provides a smooth curve linking the points where you've clicked. A variety of other options are also offered in the 'Shapes' menu, shown in Figure A40.

**Figure A40  The Shapes menu**

If you want to adjust the lines on a freehand drawing, you can do so by moving the cursor over the relevant part until it turns into a star ✢ , and then right-click and select '*Edit Points*' from the shortcut menu. Sections of the line can be dragged and dropped into place; *Word* automatically curves the adjacent sections to fit. This is particularly useful for fiddly pictures where it is important to be accurate with the alignment of different components, for example where data are graphically represented as in the illustration shown in Figure A41. '*Edit Points*' can also be obtained through the 'Insert Shapes' group on the 'Format' ribbon.

The 'Arrange' group of the 'Format' ribbon provides other functions for you to orientate your drawing and to position it in the document (via '*Text Wrapping*', '*Rotate*', *Bring to Front/Back*' etc.), some of which have been discussed in previous sections. If you want the objects to be neatly aligned, '*Grid Settings*' in the 'Align'

**Figure A41  Editing points on a drawing**

menu is a useful facility. This gives the option of 'snapping' the object to other objects or to a grid, the horizontal and vertical spacing of which are adjustable. You can choose whether the grid should be visible while editing. The benefits of using a grid are discussed further in *Section B2.3*.

## A5.3  The Selection Tool for grouping objects and creating complex diagrams

If you create a drawing out of several different components and then need to reformat the whole document you may find that the different components, such as the axes, the labelling and the points on a graph, or the arrows in equations, may drift apart. To avoid this, *Word* has a 'Grouping' facility that 'ties' the different components together so they are treated as if they were just one object – they become 'grouped'.

First, you must select all the objects to be grouped by clicking on the Selection Tool icon ▷ in the 'Editing' group of the 'Home' ribbon and choosing '*Select Objects*'. The cursor changes into the Selection Tool. Click this at one 'corner' of the group to be selected and, keeping the mouse button depressed, drag the Selection Tool over all the elements you wish to keep together. A dotted rectangle will be pulled out over your

**Figure A42  Selecting objects for grouping**

diagram, as shown in Figure A42. Then, if you right-click over the border of the group (when the cursor has turned into a little arrowed cross) and select '*Grouping/Group*' from the shortcut menu, all the objects within the selection rectangle will be 'tied together' so they are treated as one object. This facility can also be achieved via 'Group' in the 'Arrange' group of the 'Format' ribbon (Figure A43). If you want to reverse this process (for example, if you want to modify one of the elements) you can do

**Figure A43
Grouping objects**

so using '*Ungroup*'. To group successfully, you must ensure that you have enclosed all the margins of the different elements. Quite complicated diagrams and molecular structures can be produced using the drawing facility as illustrated in Figure A44.

---

**Note**

Remember to return the selection arrow back to the normal cursor, with its normal functions, at the end of this process by deselecting it (i.e. clicking again on the '*Select Objects*' button).

---

**Figure A44  Molecular structures drawn in *Word***

## A5.4  And finally – fancy text

When you insert WordArt, the 'Format' ribbon changes to offer you a range of extra facilities that allow you to alter the colour, shape and outlines. Explore these options for yourself, but remember not to go beyond the bounds of acceptability in reports that you will submit for assessment.

# A6 Macros

Macros are short computer programs that you create to perform repetitive tasks rapidly and accurately and, when you are working on long documents, a potentially very time-consuming task can become extremely quick and simple. For example, a long sequence of nucleotide bases can quickly be divided up into groups of three, with each group separated by a space (to identify the amino acid sequence). Another handy use of macros is to apply formatting throughout a document, such as changing every occurrence of a binomial name of an organism from normal to italic script. Running that macro is much quicker than finding the text using the "search" facility (described in *Section A2.7*) then changing each one manually. *Section A6.3.2* shows how you can create such macros.

When you create a macro you are actually 'writing' a computer program in *Visual Basic*, the details of which are beyond the scope of this book. You do not need to learn this programming language in order to use macros successfully, but those of you who are interested to find out more should consult a more detailed text. You will probably need to explore for yourself what you can do using macros and do remember that the Help facility in *Word* is useful for extra information. It is also worth noting that macros can be used in all other programs in the *Microsoft Office* suite.

## A6.1 Creating a macro

Macros are created by 'recording' the sequence of actions you make using successive keyboard keys and toolbar facilities. Note that operations using the mouse are not always recognized when recording macros, so you may have to find alternative routes to your end result. You start the recording process via '*View/Macro/Record Macro...*', which takes you to the 'Record Macro' dialogue box shown in Figure A45. After giving your

**Figure A45 The Record Macro dialogue box**

macro a name (use something descriptive that will remind you what it does) you must assign it to a shortcut keyboard key combination so that you are able to command *Word* to start running the macro. In Figure A45 the keyboard option is being selected – this is often the most convenient and quickest way of starting a macro. This takes you to the 'Customize Keyboard' dialogue box (Figure A46) where you assign your shortcut key combination to the macro. Many of the key combinations have already been pre-assigned (examples can be seen in Table A1 in *Section A2.2*), so you will need to try out a few to discover which ones are still available. In Figure A46 you can see that the combination **'Alt+P'** was selected for the Triplet macro.

Having assigned your shortcut combination, the cursor changes to a mini-cassette 🗄️ and from this point on, *Word* records all the actions you make using the keyboard keys until you press '*Stop Recording*' in the 'Macros' menu. If you want to pause what you are doing you can click on '*Pause Recording*'.

**Figure A46  The Customize Keyboard Dialogue Box**

## A6.2  Running the macro

Your macro is now recorded and will be retained when *Word* is shut down. It can be started each time you use the appropriate shortcut key combination and will keep on working until you assign the keyboard shortcut to another macro, in which case you will have to run

**Figure A47  The Macro dialogue box**

it from the 'Macros' dialogue box, obtained via '*View/Macros/View Macros...*', as shown in Figure A47[11]. From this dialogue box you can also create new macros, delete unwanted ones and, for those familiar with *Visual Basic*, edit existing ones.

## A6.3  Example macros

### A6.3.1  Example 1

To divide a sequence of nucleotides into groups of three, first place the cursor at the beginning of the sequence, select '*View/Macro/Record Macro...*' and assign the macro to a keyboard shortcut in the dialogue box. Then, using the right arrow key, move the cursor three spaces along the sequence and insert a space. You could, at this point, press the '*Stop Recording*' to complete the operation. Alternatively, if you

---

11  If the key combination you choose is already in use, for example **'Alt+H'**, which is the shortcut for *Home* on the main menu, you can still run your macro via the 'Macros' dialogue box.

have a really long sequence, you could make the macro do more work (so you spend less time overall) by grouping a complete line of nucleotides before stopping the recording. Now, when you place the cursor at the start of the sequence, the macro will run each time you use the keyboard shortcut, dividing text into clusters of three characters.

Applying this macro to part of the 978 sequence of nucleotides in a gene that encodes resistance to cephalosporins, converts this...

```
agtgattctttactcgcctttatcggccctcactcaaggatgtattgtggt
tatgcgttattttcgcctgtgtattatctccctgttaatgcgttattttcg
```

into this...

```
agt gat tct tta ctc gcc ttt atc ggc cct cac tca agg
atg tat tgt ggt tat gcg tta ttt tcg cct gtg tat tat
ctc cct gtt aat gcg tta ttt tcg
```

## A6.3.2 Example 2

To change all occurrences of a Latin binomial, such as Atropa belladonna (deadly nightshade), from normal to italicized script, you should place the cursor at the beginning of the document. Then, start recording your macro, not forgetting to assign a keyboard shortcut to the new macro and giving it an appropriate name. Then use the 'Find' tool (via '_Home/Find_') to locate the first occurrence of "Atropa belladonna" (but without the quote marks). Having located the text, close the 'Find' dialogue box and make sure that the text is still highlighted. Now use **'Ctrl+I'** or the font formatting dialogue box obtained via '_Home/Font_' to make the text italic (you could also use **'Alt+H/Alt+2'** in this case). Stop recording, and your macro is completed. Each time you use the keyboard shortcut combination, the cursor will move to the next occurrence in the text of "Atropa belladonna" and will change it to "_Atropa belladonna_".

# Appendix B:
## Perfect *PowerPoint*

*PowerPoint* is the *Microsoft Office* application for producing presentations. Some of its features are similar to those in *Word* and *Excel*, but others are significantly different. Many of the same options appear in the ribbons and menus (but they may be organized differently) and you can also produce your own customized 'Quick Access Toolbar' at the top of the screen using '*Office Button/PowerPoint Options/Customise*', as described in *Section A1.1*, so you can select more quickly the facilities you use most. Shortcut menus and multiple key commands can also be used. Producing a presentation, however, is very different from writing a document, and *PowerPoint* provides scope for including animation and sound. Do not get carried away with these, and always try to keep in mind what is appropriate for the audience and the context of your presentation. For example:

- try to keep slides simple and without clutter – it is less easy for the audience to pick out the important points when there is too much on display
- use one or two simple fonts that are large enough to make it easy to read (e.g. Arial or Times New Roman, and at least 18 point)
- use phrases rather than sentences, so that audiences focus on the main points
- if you want to include pictures, bear in mind that they may slow down the display
- use a background that doesn't obscure the text or diagrams

## B1 First steps in producing a *PowerPoint* presentation

*PowerPoint 2007* starts by displaying a blank 'title slide' inviting you to add a title and subtitle. If you want a different layout, perhaps to include images, an alternative can be chosen from the 'Layout' gallery, illustrated in Figure B1, by clicking on the little down arrow next to the 'Layout' icon in the 'Home' ribbon.

A wide variety of visual objects can be inserted into your slides using the 'Insert' ribbon, including tables, illustrations, text boxes, WordArt, etc. You can also insert movie and sound clips. The design of all, or individual, slides can be changed using the options available in the 'Design' ribbon shown in Figure B2.

Various built-in themes are available from the 'Theme' gallery and you can quickly assess their effect by holding the cursor over each theme: the active slide will change its appearance to match that of the theme. Further changes can be made through the '*Colors*' and '*Fonts*' menus (activated by clicking on the down-arrows adjacent to their respective buttons) in the 'Themes' group, and you can even create your own colour themes and font styles using the options at the bottom of the respective menus.

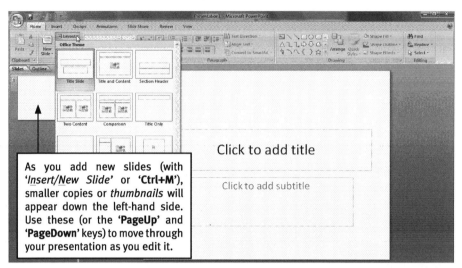

As you add new slides (with '*Insert*/*New Slide*' or '**Ctrl+M**'), smaller copies or *thumbnails* will appear down the left-hand side. Use these (or the '**PageUp**' and '**PageDown**' keys) to move through your presentation as you edit it.

**Figure B1  A Title Slide in *PowerPoint***

**Figure B2  The Design ribbon**

You can change the background colour and appearance (including variable shading if required) using the options in the 'Background' group ('*Design/Background Styles/ Format Background*'), and this facility can also set your own pictures and graphics as background.

# B2 Standard formatting in *PowerPoint*

If you decide to use one of the standard layouts presented from the 'Layout' gallery, your text size will automatically be selected for you and this will help you achieve overall consistency in your presentation. Once you have chosen a layout you can start typing into the text boxes outlined in the slide. The default manner in which *PowerPoint* organizes and formats your text is shown below.

- Text in the main body of a *PowerPoint* slide is conventionally formatted in 'bulleted lists' like this, with each paragraph forming a single 'bullet point'.
- The main bulleted list in each slide is called the 'first level'.
  - First level points often contain subordinate lists,
  - starting with the 'second level'.
    - There can also be a 'third level',
      - a 'fourth level',
        - or even a 'fifth level'.

- Notice that the bullet style differs at the different levels, and the text size gets progressively smaller, to highlight the logical structure of the slide (although you can overwrite this if you wish).

To change the level of your paragraphs to the next one down, click on the 'Increase Indent' ⊞ icon in the 'Paragraph' group of the 'Home' ribbon (or alternatively position the cursor at the start of the line and press '**Tab**'). To go up a level use the 'Decrease Indent' ⊞ icon (or '**Shift+Tab**'). You can edit the bullet style using the options available via the '*Home/Bullets*' ⊞ ▾ and '*Home/Numbering*' ⊞ ▾ icons in the 'Paragraph' group of the 'Home' ribbon and the '**Tab**' key as required. As you change each paragraph's level it will automatically be reformatted, with the font size, style, etc. being changed accordingly.

## B2.1  Using the Slide Master to set your style

If you find that *PowerPoint*'s default design (or any existing design template that you may be using) does not suit the material you wish to present, you can change it using the 'Slide Master' facility which is reached via '*View/Slide Master*'. As you do this, a 'Slide Master' tab appears on the main toolbar at the left of the 'Home' tab. You are presented with a variety of slide layouts on the left of the page from which you can choose the one most suitable.

A common 'Master' layout will look something like the picture shown in Figure B3. You can edit it more or less as if it were an individual slide, for example, by changing the bullet styles, font size and formatting (bold, italic, font type, colour, etc.), line spacing, positioning of the text boxes, etc. It is worth taking time to do this carefully, because after you have defined this Slide Master and closed it (using '*Slide Master/ Close Slide Master*'), any slides you add to your presentation will automatically be formatted in the

**Figure B3  The Slide Master**

same style. Using the Slide Master can save you large amounts of time, since if you want to adjust the style of presentation as you add to its content, or present it to different audiences, then you can change all of the slides simultaneously simply by re-editing the Slide Master.

---

**Tip**

It is a VERY good idea always to start your presentation by designing an appropriate Slide Master. *Do not* attempt to hand-edit the layout of all of your slides independently, or you will waste lots of time and probably end up with an inconsistent mess instead of a nicely polished presentation.

### B2.1.1 Adding pagination, footers and background images

You can also use the Slide Master to place page numbers, footers, logos or background images, etc. on all of your slides automatically. If you do add a background image (through '*Slide Master/Background*') you will need to force it *behind* any text boxes; do this by right-clicking on the image, then selecting '*Send to Back*' from the shortcut menu. By setting a high percentage transparency you can ensure that your background does not dominate your slides.

## B2.2 Creating new slides using the standard layout

As you add new slides to your presentation ('*Home/New Slide*' or '**Ctrl+M***'), it will automatically be assigned the layout of the Master Slide, but you can choose a different layout from the slide layout gallery ('*Home/Layout*') pictured in Figure B1. It is simplest to select the one closest to what you intend initially and then modify it later if you need to. The layouts offered include some that allow you to insert graphs, charts, tables, *Clip Art* and even some sound effects and

**Figure B4  A standard layout**

animations, as shown in Figure B4. You can also insert an exact copy of the previous slide via '*Home/New Slide/Duplicate Selected Slide*' which you can then edit.

## B2.3 Creating slides 'freehand'

If you would rather not use the standard layouts for your slides, you can choose the 'Blank' slide option in the 'Layout' gallery and then insert a variety of different objects into slides in much the same way as you can in *Word*, using the '*Insert*' ribbon (pictured in Figure B5). This makes provision for inserting slide numbers, date, time, pictures, diagrams, charts and tables, and also movies and sounds.

**Figure B5  The Insert ribbon**

### B2.3.1 Adding text to your 'freehand' slides

When it comes to adding text that is not automatically set using the Master Slide, *PowerPoint* and *Word* differ far more significantly. To put text into *PowerPoint*, you must first insert a text box.

> **Note:** all text in *PowerPoint* is contained within text boxes.

Text boxes are inserted using '*Insert/Text Box*', or by clicking on the text box icon A in the 'Insert' ribbon, and they can then be manipulated to give the effects you want. The 'Home' ribbon automatically appears when you type into a text box, making available the 'Font' group that contains all the font formatting facilities (such as bold/italic/underline/colour, etc.) that can be found in *Microsoft Word*. The 'Paragraph' area of the ribbon, however, gives slightly fewer options for formatting paragraphs than are available in *Word*. Do remember that these facilities can also be reached, perhaps more quickly, via the right-click shortcut menus.

The 'Home' menu also includes an 'Editing' group which, in a similar manner to *Word*, allows you to search for ('*Home/Find*') and replace words ('*Home/Replace*') and also to systematically alter fonts ('*Home/Replace/Replace Fonts*').

It is far more difficult to achieve a tidy and uniform 'look and feel' to your presentations if you are creating it freehand because if you are not careful each slide may have different sizes of text boxes with a variety of spacings, colours and fonts. The best way of avoiding this is to use a Slide Master. If you do need to create your slides freehand, however, it would be a good idea to use the 'Snap objects to grid' facility (through '*Home/Arrange/Align/Grid Settings*') to make objects and text boxes line up neatly. This is discussed more fully in *Section B8.3*.

# B3  Inserting hyperlinks

Adding hyperlinks to your presentation can give you access to a much wider variety of information to illustrate your topic and thus make the slide show more interesting. Links can be made to other files on your computer or to material on the web. There are two ways in which you can do this, either by inserting hyperlinks as text within sentences or labels, or as Action Buttons.

## B3.1  Inserting hyperlinks as text and images

To create the hyperlink, select the text or the image you wish to act as the link (The Biochemical Society, in the example shown here), then click '*Insert/Hyperlink*', or right-click to use the shortcut menu and select the '*Hyperlink*' option. A box will appear similar to that pictured in Figure B6. If you selected text for the hyperlink the '*Text to display*' window will contain that portion of text,

**Figure B6  Inserting hyperlinks**

whereas if you selected an object or image it will contain ‹‹Selection in document››. You are asked to insert the web address for your link into the '*Address*' window, which can be the file name browsed from your computer or a Web address (in this example, http://www.biochemistry.org/). The text in your slide for this link will then appear in a different colour and will become active once the slide show is running (not while you are editing it).

Providing you have the appropriate software that supports animations on your computer, hyperlinks to animations on the internet can be effective – but do make sure, beforehand, that the computer which you will use for your presentation can run these animations.

## B3.2  Using Action Buttons for hyperlinks, shortcuts to other files and for sound effects

Action Buttons such as these ◀ ▶ can be inserted into a slide when you choose from the 'Action Buttons' options (shown in Figure B7) at the bottom of the 'Shapes' menu (seen via '*Insert/Shapes*'). Once you've selected a button and drawn it on the slide (dragging it out to an appropriate size), the 'Action Settings' dialogue box pictured in Figure B8 appears, inviting you to set its function. Selecting the 'Hyperlink' option allows you to link to other sites, including another slide in your show (if you do not want to run through it in numerical order). This might be useful if you want to retain all the original slides in

**Figure B7  The Action Button menu**

their original order, but skip some slides to suit different audiences (although there are better ways of doing this as described in Section B5.2). Another option provided by the 'Action Settings' dialogue box is to include sounds. Some are provided, including applause, cash register and explosions, but you can also insert a variety of other noises, such as recordings of musical tracks or animal calls, from external sources. Depending on which option is used in the dialogue box, Action Buttons can be activated either when the mouse cursor simply moves over the button (Mouse Over) or by positioning the cursor over it and clicking the mouse.

**Figure B8  The Action Settings dialogue box**

# B4 Animation effects

The animation effects possible in *PowerPoint* can help your presentation appear lively and interesting, but to be effective you MUST be careful not to overdo them because they can easily detract from the main thrust of the talk and make it look gimmicky rather than polished. It takes time to become familiar with all the available animations, but it is worth spending some time on them because when done carefully they can make the finished presentation look very sophisticated.

## B4.1 *Creating the animations*

'*Animations/Animate*' and '*Animations/Custom Animation*' offer a variety of different effects for animating text and objects, from the mild, such as fading in or out, to the outlandish, where the text or objects bounce or boomerang about. These can be applied to all the slides or to individual ones. The best way of learning about these is to create a simple presentation, then try applying some of them in turn and see what happens when you play the slide show, using either '*Slide Show/From Beginning*', '*Slide Show/From Current Slide*', the shortcut key '**F5**', or by clicking the 'Slide Show' icon 🖵 at the bottom of the screen.

If you want to animate individual text boxes, images or other objects in your presentation, it is possible to do so using the 'Custom Animation' task pane which when activated (through '*Animations/Custom Animation*') appears on the right of the main window. '*Add Effect*' on this task pane, pictured in Figure B9, allows you to define how the object appears ('*Entrance*')

**Figure B9 Adding animation effects**

and disappears ('*Exit*'), and also provides options for special effects ('*Emphasis*') and movement across the screen ('*Motion Path*'). You can set the timing of the effect by either clicking on the down-arrow to the right of the 'Start' window and choosing the appropriate option from the drop-down menu or, alternatively, clicking on the actual animation instruction in the task pane, as shown in Figure B10, and selecting the down-arrow that appears to the right of the instruction. Both of these activate a sub-menu, which allows you to set such things as a delay before the animation occurs and the number of times the effect is repeated, etc. There is also an option to remove the animation effect. Remember to check how your animations appear in individual slides using the

**Figure B10 Timing effects**

'Play' and 'Start Show' buttons at the bottom of the task pane (and also found in the 'Start Slide Show' group in the 'Slide Show' ribbon).

### B4.1.1 Keeping track of the animation instructions

Helpfully, the 'Custom Animation' task pane accumulates a list of the various animation instructions in their chronological order, illustrated in Figure B11, so you can easily identify which animations have been applied to particular objects and in what order they occur. By dragging an animation instruction up and down the list you can quickly change the order in which it occurs. You can also modify any animation effect either by right-clicking the mouse over it and choosing the appropriate modification from the sub-menu, or, as described in the previous paragraph, by left-clicking on the animation instruction and then clicking on the down-arrow next to it to activate the relevant sub-menu.

**Figure B11  An animation list**

### B4.1.2 Imported animations

Animations in the form of animated GIF files can be inserted directly into your presentation in the same way as you would insert a normal image file into a document ('*Insert/Picture*').

### B4.1.3 Using entrance animations to build a slide bit by bit

Sometimes you might want to add successive elements to a slide, for example, by adding a sequence of bullet points to a list, or adding labels to a diagram in a consecutive manner. Rather than creating a new slide for each new addition, it is far more efficient to produce just one slide containing all of the elements together. You can then add an entrance animation to each of them so that successive elements appear after repeated clicks of the mouse or after some specified time delay, with each of the elements being revealed in turn. Doing this keeps your presentation more tidy and also reduces the size of the file.

## B4.2 Moving through your slides

### B4.2.1 Setting the slide transitions

You can obtain a variety of visual effects for leading from one slide to the next during the presentation by using the facilities in the 'Transition to this Slide' group in the 'Animation' ribbon. By clicking on the down-arrow next to the gallery of options

**Figure B12  The Slide Transition group**

(Figure B12), you will be presented with a larger selection of transitions from which to choose. The 'Animation' ribbon also allows you to set the speed of each transition and the timing, for example, after a mouse-click or after a time lag. These can be applied to individual slides or to all the slides in the presentation (using the 'Apply to All' button). In general, it is best to use the same sort of transition throughout unless you have a specific reason for varying it.

# B5 Organizing your presentation

The '*View*' ribbon (Figure B13) is particularly important in helping you to order the slides and to check that the presentation runs as you expect. '*Normal*' shows the standard screen when you are producing the slides, with thumbnails down the left-hand side and slide layout/design, etc. on the right. You can drag

**Figure B13  The Slide Sorter**

and drop the thumbnails to change the order of the slides, but it is awkward to do this if you are moving the slides a long way. Therefore, it is best to select the '*Slide Sorter*' view, either from the ribbon or more quickly by clicking on the 'Slide Sorter View' icon in the bottom right-hand side of the screen, as shown in Figure B14. This shows thumbnails over the entire screen, making it much easier to reposition them. This view can also be very useful for giving an overview of the presentation, to make sure it has a coherent shape.

To get back to the edit screen, select '*View/Normal*' or click on the 'Normal' icon ⊞. To view the finished slide show, select '*View/Slide Show*', click on the 'Slide Show' icon ⬚ or press the shortcut key '**F5**'.

**Figure B14  Quick access to Slide Sorter**

# B6 Giving your presentation

## B6.1 Using the keyboard keys to move through slides

When showing a presentation, the left mouse button is generally used to move forward from slide to slide, though the ↓, →, '**Enter**' and '**PageDown**' keys have a similar effect. To move backwards through the slides, use instead the ↑, ←, '**Backspace**' or '**PageUp**' keys.

## B6.2 Tailor your presentation to your audience by skipping or omitting slides

If you decide that you want to omit a particular slide when showing your presentation to a particular audience, you do not have to delete it permanently; simply select the slide and then use '*Slide Show/Hide Slide*'. You can also skip backwards and forwards between slides that are not adjacent to each other, perhaps to emphasize a particular point more than once, by entering the number of the slide you want to go to and then pressing the '**Return**' key. Remember, however, that you will need to know the number of each slide and/or have a printed summary of the presentation in front of you to do this efficiently!

# B7 Printing handouts

You can create handouts from your slides in a variety of formats. The easiest way to do this is through '*View/ Handout Master*' where you can specify the overall layout and orientation of the slides and also the size of the paper. If you want the handouts to

**Figure B15  Printing the presentation**

have specific headers or footers, the best way is by using '*View/Handout Master*'. To print the handouts use '*Office Button/Print*' ('**Alt+F/Alt+P**'). The 'Print' dialogue box that appears also gives options for organizing the slides as illustrated in Figure B15. Remember, also, that you can use the '*Properties*' (and perhaps also the '*Finishing*') button to set the printing on both sides of the paper. Make sure that you check the layout using '*Office Button/Print/Print Preview*' before committing yourself to print!

# B8  Using *PowerPoint* for posters

The facilities provided in *PowerPoint* can make it easy to create scientific posters but, due to the much larger size of the finished product, there are several important points that you should bear in mind as you construct your poster.

## B8.1  Setting the poster size

Your poster will be large – usually A0 size (but do check the size requirement or restrictions before you start) which means that images that look fine on your PC monitor or printed on an A4-sized sheet may become indistinct once blown up to the final size.

**Figure B16  The Page Setup dialogue box**

So before doing anything else, you should set the size of the finished poster in the 'Page Setup' dialogue box (Figure B16) via '*Design/Page Setup*', and then, in the '*Slides sized for*' window, choose '*Custom*'. You can then enter the appropriate width and height of your poster. Standard sizes are shown in Table B1.

**Table B1  Standard paper dimensions**

| Size | Dimensions (cm) |
|------|-----------------|
| A0 | 84.1 × 118.9 |
| A1 | 59.4 × 84.1 |
| A2 | 42.0 × 59.4 |
| A3 | 29.7 × 42.0 |

You should also set the orientation (portrait or landscape) according to the space allowed for the poster. Remember that you will need to define a margin around the poster because printers often do not print right to the edge of the slide.

## B8.2 Adding components to your poster

You can then create your poster by adding text (in text boxes), images, charts, and so on, as if you were creating slides 'freehand' as described in *Section B2.3*. Because it is a much larger presentation you should make sure the main text is large (20–28 point) so it is easily readable from a distance of a metre, with larger fonts for sub-headings and titles (36–54 point). WordArt can be used for impact for the main heading, but remember not to make it too fussy! Above all, you should aim for clarity.

If you want to include images make sure their file extensions are recognized by *PowerPoint*. Such files include EMF, GIF, JPEG, PNG and BMP. If you scan an image, the resolution should be high enough to give adequate definition even when the image is enlarged to poster size; otherwise it will appear ill-defined and fuzzy.

## B8.3 Aligning the components of your poster

It is particularly important to line up the various elements of your poster to give a neat and attractive appearance. The 'Snap objects to grid' facility (mentioned previously in *Section B2.3.1*) helps you to do this and can be reached through '*Home/Arrange/Align/Grid Settings*'. This activates the 'Grid and Guides' dialogue box, as pictured in Figure B17. Through this you can select the '*Display grid on screen*' option if you want to see a grid (although it is also possible to achieve this via '*View/Gridlines*'), and by selecting '*Snap objects to grid*',

**Figure B17 The Grid and Guides dialogue box**

any objects you add will automatically become aligned to the grid. You can also create on-screen guidelines, illustrated in Figure B18, by selecting the '*Display drawing guides on screen*' option. More guidelines can be created if you place the cursor over one of the guides and hold down the '**Ctrl**' key while dragging it to a different position.

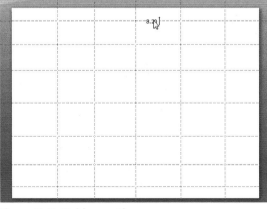

**Figure B18 Guides on the screen**

# Appendix C:
## Easy and effective *Excel*

You may already have some experience of using *Excel* for organizing data and handling calculations and might be familiar with the information in the first few sections. There may, however, be some shortcuts and functions described in them which you have not yet explored, so it is still worth reading through these sections. The later sections cover the facilities concerned with formatting, performing calculations and also for portraying your data in a variety of graphical forms. By the end, you will be equipped to take advantage of *Excel* to organize and display your data in a form that is clear and looks polished.

The main aims of this section are to improve your understanding of how to:

- insert data into a spreadsheet and format it appropriately
- perform routine calculations (editing the formulae when necessary)
- display data clearly as graphs or charts

The Tabbed Main Menu of *Excel 2007* has several features in common with *Word* and *PowerPoint,* but there are also many additional facilities specific to *Excel*. Shortcut menus and multiple key commands offer a quick route to many of the facilities and these will be represented by the same notation as that described in *Section A1.2*, so make sure you have read that section before trying to understand what follows.

## C1 Workbooks, worksheets and cells

When you open a new *Excel* file, the main window shows an empty spreadsheet called a 'worksheet', with a grid of labelled columns and rows, illustrated in Figure C1.

**Figure C1 A new Excel spreadsheet**

Each column is automatically assigned a letter and each row a number, which allows you to specify each individual cell (columns always come before rows, such as A3 or D7). When using an *Excel* spreadsheet, most of the time there will be only one 'active' or selected cell which is the 'working' area in which data can be changed. This appears with a darker border than the other cells and a small dark square in the bottom right-hand corner. The 'Address' of that cell is shown in the 'Name' box at the top left hand of the 'Formula' bar. A cell can be selected (activated) either by moving the cursor over the cell and then clicking or by using the arrow keys to select a different active cell. The cursor will change into a chunky cross, pictured in Figure C2, and the contents of that cell will appear in the 'Formula' bar.

**Figure C2  Cell selection**

More worksheets may be added to this *Excel* file via '*Home/Insert/Insert Sheet*', (or '**Shift+F11**') and each one can be assigned its own name by right-clicking over the assigned 'Name' tab at the bottom left of the sheet (shown in Figure C3) and choosing '*Rename*'. You can move between different worksheets by clicking on the appropriate 'Name' tab. Having several worksheets within one workbook allows you to copy data from one to another relatively easily and also means that when you save a workbook, all the spreadsheets contained within that workbook will be saved into the same file.

**Figure C3  The Name tabs**

# C2  Entering and editing data

If you have a lot of results to put into a spreadsheet, you can save time by picking the most appropriate way of entering and editing the data. The following sections will give you ideas of how to become more efficient at doing this.

## C2.1  Entering data

To enter new data into an *Excel* spreadsheet, click on the cell in which you wish to enter the first value and then type it in. The characters appear in the cell and also next to the symbol $f_x$ in the 'Formula' bar across the top of the spreadsheet. To 'fix' the data in the cell (so it doesn't disappear if, by mistake, you click on the Escape key or the red cross in the 'Formula' bar) you must either click on another cell or press the '**Return**' (or '**Enter**') key or one of the arrow keys, or click on the tick that appears in the 'Formula' bar $\times \checkmark f_x$ . Choose whichever option is quickest for the way you are entering data. For example, if you are typing a series of numbers into a column, the '**Return**' key will be easiest to use, whereas if you are entering data into different parts of the spreadsheet, using the mouse to select the cells may be quickest.

When working with a very large spreadsheet that does not fit entirely onto the screen, it is often convenient to 'split' the screen using *'View/Split'*. This causes the spreadsheet to become divided into two vertical and two horizontal portions, with the ability to scroll along each portion independently of the others. If you want to stop a selected portion of the spreadsheet from moving completely, for example, the top row or first column, you can do this using the options available in *'View/ Freeze Panes'*. By doing this, it is easier to see the relative positions of the cells into which you enter your data.

### C2.1.1 Transferring data from Word documents into Excel spreadsheets (and vice versa)

You can easily import data into *Excel* spreadsheets from data contained in tables in *Word* documents. Select the table, or part of the table, that you want, and copy it to the Clipboard using **'Ctrl+C'** or *'Copy'* from the shortcut menu, then open an *Excel* workbook. *Providing it does not interfere with other existing data in the spreadsheet*, select a cell which you want to appear at the top left of the pasted data table and then use **'Ctrl+V'** or *'Paste'* from the shortcut menu. (Note: when you right-click the mouse, a small formatting menu appears simultaneously with the shortcut menu so you can quickly make additional formatting changes if you wish.) If an information box appears stating that the data in the clipboard are a different size and shape from the selected cells and asking whether you want to go ahead and paste the data anyway, click 'OK' and your data will appear in the spreadsheet.

To transfer data from Excel spreadsheets into a Word document, simply select the part of the worksheet or the chart you wish to transfer, then use **'Ctrl+C'** or *'Copy'* to put it into the Clipboard. Open the *Word* document into which you wish to paste the information, place the cursor in an appropriate position and use **'Ctrl+V'**. The data or chart will be reproduced as a table in *Word* format.

### C2.1.2 Transferring data from the internet

Data can be also transported from the Internet into *Excel* but you must ensure that the data are 'tidy' beforehand. To check this, paste the data into a *Word* table first and use the 'Show/Hide' ¶ icon to see how the data are formatted and remove anything that *Excel* would not recognize, such as hypertext tags involving '⟨' and '⟩' characters. Using the editing facility *'Home/Replace'* (**'Ctrl+H'**) facility should help speed up the process.

Options for importing data from other sources such as *Access* databases are provided in the 'Data' ribbon.

## C2.2 Replacing or correcting data in a cell

Data in a cell are replaced automatically if you enter a new value into that cell which makes it quick and easy to amend mistakes. Be careful, therefore, that you check before entering a new value that it is going into the correct cell. If you do enter data into a cell by mistake but have not yet finalized the entry, you can return to the previous contents by clicking on the red cross that appears in the 'Formula' bar. Otherwise you will need to use the 'Undo' facility (**'Ctrl+Z'**).

If you wish to alter, but not completely replace, data in a cell you must do this by editing the text in the 'Formula' bar. First, make the cell active, then click over the 'Formula' bar. The cursor will change shape and you can then edit the cell contents as you would for word processing in *Word*. Do remember to finalize the change afterwards.

## C2.3 Numeric formats

*Excel* may present numbers to many more decimal places than you require. This can easily be adjusted using the 'Decrease Decimal' icon (see Figure C4) in the 'Number' group of the 'Home' ribbon. After selecting the cells containing the data you wish to modify, click on the icon. The number of decimal places will decrease by one for each click

**Figure C4 The Decrease Decimal icon**

and the displayed value will also be rounded appropriately. Conversely, if you want to increase the number of decimal places shown, you can use the adjacent 'Increase Decimal' icon. You can display numbers in a variety of different forms via the 'Format Cells' dialogue box, which appears when you click on the arrow in the bottom right-hand side of the 'Number' group. By selecting '*Custom*' from the list displayed, you can choose an appropriate notation from those provided. Table C1 shows how the top row of numbers can be displayed when *Excel* is instructed to apply the scientific notations shown in the first column.

**Table C1 Numeric notations**

| Notation offered | Numerical Value | | | |
|---|---|---|---|---|
| | 0.005678 | 5.67809 | 5678.91 | 56789123.4 |
| 0.00 | 0.01 | 5.68 | 5678.91 | 56789123.40 |
| #,##0 | 0 | 6 | 5,679 | 56,789,123 |
| #,##0.00 | 0.01 | 5.68 | 5,678.91 | 56,789,123.40 |
| 0.00% | 0.57% | 567.81% | 567891.00% | 5678912340.00% |
| 0.00E+00 | 5.68E-03 | 5.68E+00 | 5.68E+03 | 5.68E+07 |
| ##0.0E+0 | 5.7E-3 | 5.7E+0 | 5.7E+3 | 56.8E+6 |

The '0' indicates a position in which a digit will be forced to appear, even if it is a leading or a trailing zero, '#' indicates a position in which a digit will appear only if it is significant (so leading and trailing zeros will be ignored) and ',' indicates that commas should be inserted in appropriate places to group digits into thousands/ millions/billions, etc.

## C2.4 Operations on blocks of cells

Although only one cell can be made active at a time, and the data in it changed by typing, several cells may be selected together for a general operation such as copying or clearing of data or formatting changes (discussed in *Section C4*). To

**Figure C5 Selecting several cells together**

select several cells, make sure the cursor is a chunky cross, then click in one of the corner cells of the area you want to select, and drag the mouse over the required area. The selected cells will become pale blue (illustrated in Figure C5) and you can then right-click to obtain the shortcut menu containing operations that you may wish to perform. As in *Word*, not all of the options may be visible in this menu and you may need to go to the ribbons to find what you want. If you wish to perform an operation on the entire grid, such as copying all the data or sorting all the data with respect to one column, click the cursor in the top left-hand corner of the chart.

# C3 Performing calculations

*Excel* can perform many different calculations and each of these requires a specific formula, some examples of which are shown in Table C2. The appropriate formula must be inserted into the cell in which you want the answer to appear. Since *cell* locations are specified, rather than the values that they contain, if you change the numerical value within a cell that is specified in a formula, the result is automatically recalculated.

All the formulae start with an equals sign '=' so *Excel* knows that a formula is being entered rather than just text. Table C2 lists the notation for some common calculations. In many cases you may not need to type these in manually because *Excel* has appropriate shortcut buttons (described in the following section), but it is worth knowing them because you are likely to need to make adjustments to your formulae, or to the range of cells to which they apply.

> **Note**
>
> If you do actually want to enter text preceded by '=', you must type an apostrophe before the '=' to let *Excel* know it is not a formula.

**Table C2 Some common formulae used by *Excel***

| Symbol | Example | Function |
|---|---|---|
| + | =(B2+F3+25) | Adds |
| - | =(B4-D2-5) | Subtracts |
| / | =(D9/A2)/100 | Divides |
| * | =(B7*C3) | Multiplies (remember not to use 'x', which is just a letter not a mathematical symbol in *Excel*) |
| SUM | =SUM(A2:A25) | Adds the range of cells specified (in this example, all the cells from A2 to A25) |
| AVERAGE | =AVERAGE(A2:A25) | Calculates the mean value of the range of cells specified (A2 to A25) |
| STDEV | =STDEV(A2:A25) | Calculates the standard deviation of the range of cells specified (A2 to A25) |
| ^ | =A5^3 | Raises the value specified to the power of whatever number appears to the right of the symbol (in this example, A5 would be cubed) |

## C3.1 *Entering your formulae*

To enter a function, the cell in which the result is to appear must first be made active and the appropriate formula then entered into this cell. Helpfully, 'AutoSum' in the 'Formulas' ribbon provides a list of functions for the most commonly used calculations (shown in Figure C6) so that you do not have to type them into the 'Formula' bar yourself. When using the Autosum facility you must make sure you *hold down the* '**Ctrl**' *key as you choose the function*. Then you should release the '**Ctrl**' key before clicking on the first cell you want to include

**Figure C6 The Autosum menu**

in your formula, and finally you must hold down the '**Ctrl**' key again as you select additional cells you want to include in the calculation. To select adjacent cells you can simply drag the mouse over them. You will see the cell positions being added to the 'Formula' bar as you do this. To finalize your set of data, press the '**Return**' key and your result will appear in the chosen cell.

If the function you want is not displayed, for example, standard deviation, you will need to select '*More Functions*'. This provides a further list of possibilities, illustrated in Figure C7. If, again, your function is not listed, you can search for it in the '*Search for a function*' box. Having chosen the one you want (holding down the '**Ctrl**' key as you do so), a 'Function Arguments' dialogue box, pictured in Figure C8, will appear, with a suggested range of cells in the 'Number 1' window to which the function will apply. Click 'OK' and this range of cells

**Figure C7 The Insert Function dialogue box**

will appear in the 'Formula' bar. *At this point you should release the* '**Ctrl**' *key*. The range of cells often needs to be edited. You can do this by editing directly in the 'Function Arguments' dialogue box, or in the 'Formula' bar, using the '**Delete**' or

**Figure C8 The Function Arguments dialogue box**

'**Backspace**' keys and typing in the amendments. However, sometimes a quicker way is to select the first cell to be included in the formula and then hold down the '**Ctrl**' key while you make your further selections, as described previously. Once all the appropriate cells have been selected press the '**OK**' button to finalize the result.

> **Note**
>
> If you do not select the cell in which you want to display the calculated result, *Excel* will automatically put it adjacent to the last cell in the row or column of data. You can, however, move the calculated result (together with its associated formula) to another cell if, after selecting the cell containing the result, you move the cursor over it until a little 'arrowed' cross appears as shown in Figure C9. You can then hold down the left-hand mouse button as you drag the cell to another position.

**Figure C9 The arrowed cross**

*Excel* provides an enormous range of useful functions, many of which require the specification of a complicated sequence of 'arguments' or 'parameters' (entered using the 'Function Arguments' box). It is not possible to cover these here, but if you know enough about the function to use it you should find *Excel*'s help facilities very useful. To use these, click on the '*Help on this function*' link at the bottom left of the 'Function Arguments' box.

## C3.1.1 Error messages

If there are problems with the formula you have entered, or some of the data don't fit appropriately into the formula, *Excel* will produce an error message. You should then check why *Excel* has shown the message and correct the formula or the data as required. If the message appears because the range of cells specified by the formula includes a cell that itself contains an error, you can replace the error code in that one cell by an asterisk, and then proceed with the others as normal. Some of the most common error messages are shown in Table C3.

**Table C3 Common error messages**

| Error code | Meaning |
|---|---|
| #### | The cell is too narrow to display the contents – make the column wider. See *Section C4.2.1* for how to do this |
| #DIV/0 | The formula is trying to divide by zero – check that the formula is correct and that you are not instructing the formula to divide by cells containing zero (in this context, blank cells are treated as zero by *Excel*) |
| #NAME | *Excel* doesn't recognize a name used in the formula – check your typing |
| #NUM | There is a problem with a number in your formula – check the numbers |
| #REF | The formula uses a cell reference that is not valid – check that you have specified a suitable range of cells and that their names are correct |
| #VALUE | You have used the wrong type of number or have attempted to calculate using a cell containing text – check your typing and the specific cells |

## C3.1.2 Saving time with calculations – spreading formulae

*Excel* has a very useful 'Autofill' function which allows you to 'spread' a formula to adjacent cells. This means that a calculation performed using one set of cells can be automatically applied to a range of others, without you needing to type in formula for each successive set of data. For example, if you want the mean values of each of several rows of data, you can perform the function on the first row, putting the result in a cell at the end and then 'spread' the formula down the column, as shown below. Make sure you check in the 'Formula' bar that the cell range suggested by *Excel* is correct each time.

To spread the formula, first select the cell containing the formula you want to spread, and then move the mouse pointer over the small square in the corner of the selection. The pointer will change into a thin 'selection' cross as shown in Figure C10. When this happens, hold down the left mouse button and drag it over the cells to which you wish to spread the formula or data. When you release the button,

**Figure C10 The selection cross**

the cells will automatically be filled. Figure C11 shows how the mean value of the first set of data from four trials (cells A2 to D2) has been averaged in column F, and the formula '=AVERAGE(A2:D2)' has been spread down column F so the mean result has been calculated for all the sets of data. You can check that the formula has 'spread' correctly by selecting any of the filled cells in column F and looking in the 'Formula' bar at the range of cells used in the formula. This 'spreading' method can also be used for filling in successive numbers, dates or times. For example, if you type 'Monday' into a cell, spreading the 'formula' will cause successive cells to be filled with 'Tuesday', 'Wednesday', 'Thursday', and so on. Alternatively, if you want to number a long column of items, put '1' in the cell to the left of the first item, '2' in the cell below that, then select these two cells, click on the 'cross' icon and drag down the column: successive cells will be filled with '3', '4', '5', etc.

pH enzyme 2

|   | A | B | C | D | E | F |
|---|---|---|---|---|---|---|
| 1 | Trial 1 | Trial 2 | Trial 3 | Trial 4 | | |
| 2 | 62.38 | 55.42 | 57.81 | 62.88 | | 59.6225 |
| 3 | 67.57 | 43.61 | 64.77 | 67.49 | | 60.86 |
| 4 | 71.51 | 51.71 | 62.96 | 59.98 | | 61.54 |
| 5 | 81.14 | 49.74 | 59.09 | 63.86 | | 63.4575 |
| 6 | 83.38 | 53.43 | 63.52 | 66.79 | | 66.78 |
| 7 | 57.97 | 53.62 | 69.64 | 57.79 | | 59.755 |
| 8 | 69.01 | 56.45 | 73.28 | 61.35 | | 65.0225 |
| 9 | 77.52 | 67.83 | 65.47 | 68.31 | | 69.7825 |
| 10 | 74.92 | 58.59 | 63.91 | 71.02 | | 67.11 |
| 11 | 69.92 | 54.88 | 58.87 | 67.52 | | 62.7975 |
| 12 | 76.65 | 52.31 | 70.21 | 64.76 | | 65.9825 |
| 13 | 76.15 | 60.59 | 68.43 | 73.07 | | 69.56 |

**Figure C11 Spreading a formula**

## C3.1.3 Transferring calculated data within and between spreadsheets

When formulae are copied (or cut) and pasted from one cell to another, they are automatically adjusted to operate on corresponding cells, in the same way as when they are spread. So, for example, when a formula in cell F2 that gives the sum of cells A2 to D2 is copied to cell F8, the numerical value in F8 will be the sum of cells A8 to D8. This means that you cannot just copy columns of calculated values to another part of the spreadsheet or to a different spreadsheet, since those values will change. *Excel* provides a solution to this problem through the 'Paste Special' facility. If you want to copy (or move) a set of calculated results, rather than the formulae themselves, first select and copy (or cut) the relevant cells to the Clipboard, then move to the new position and select '*Home/Paste/Paste Special/Values*' (or choose '*Paste Special*' from the shortcut menu). Another way to do this is to paste the calculated data first into a *Word* document (which doesn't attach the formulae to the numbers) as described in *Section C2.1.1* and then transfer it all back into a new *Excel* worksheet.

# C4 Formatting spreadsheets

The appearance of a spreadsheet can affect the ease with which the data can be understood, so it is worth spending a bit of time ensuring that it is well ordered and the data well spaced with appropriate headings (and charts).

## C4.1 *Sorting your data*

Once you have your data and any calculations finalized, you may wish to rearrange the final calculated values, perhaps in alphabetical order or with the highest or lowest first. *Excel* is able to perform this task on whole worksheets or on selected ranges of data via the 'Sort & Filter' group in the 'Data' ribbon (see Figure C12), followed by the 'Sort' dialogue box illustrated in

**Figure C12 The Sort & Filter group**

Figure C13. You can also get to the 'Sort' dialogue box through the 'Editing' group in the 'Home' ribbon, but this route via '*Custom Sort*' is slightly longer.

Remember that when selecting the entire worksheet, it is easiest to do this by clicking the box in its top left-hand corner. Choose the column you want to reorder by clicking the down-arrow next to the 'Sort by' window. If you have selected the '*My data has headers*' option, *Excel* will use the column names; otherwise it will simply give the letter heading the column. Where columns contain numbers, text or dates and times, the 'Sort On' window should be set to 'Values'. You should then decide how you want to sort by selecting the appropriate command from the 'Order' window, for example in alphabetical or increasing numerical order.

You can refine the arrangement of your data by adding extra levels of organization within the initial order when you select '*Add Level*'. This allows data to be subdivided into more easily viewed groups of

**Figure C13 The Sort dialogue box**

information. This has been done in Figure C13, where three levels of organization have been chosen with the overall order dependent upon Column B, and subsequently ordered by Column I and then by Column D. If your data are organized in rows, use the '*Options*' button to reset the dialogue box.

---

**Warning:** when sorting data make absolutely sure that you have selected everything that is to be included in the sort. If you do not you are very likely to find that different bits of information related to the same set of data will be assigned to different rows and your spreadsheet will become very muddled! It is very easy, for example, mistakenly to sort a single column such that all data in that column change position, but their corresponding entries in other columns remain unaltered, usually making a nonsense of your spreadsheet.

---

## C4.2 Formatting rows and columns

**Figure C14 Selecting a row**

You can quickly format whole rows or columns by positioning the cursor in the grey areas alongside the chosen row or column. The cursor will change into a black arrow, pictured in Figure C14, and after clicking once, the whole row or column will become blue, indicating that it has been selected. By right-clicking to obtain the shortcut menu (shown in Figure C15), you can then choose the required operation. In addition to formatting the cells, you can clear their contents or delete the entire row or column. If you need extra cells, this shortcut menu also provides an option for inserting additional rows and columns. *Excel* moves all the following rows and columns along to make room for the inserted cells and any calculations relating to data in the moved cells are adapted accordingly. An alternative route to inserting rows and columns is via '*Home/Insert*'. You can clear the contents of rows and columns through '*Home/Clear*'.

**Figure C15 The Formatting shortcut menu**

### C4.2.1 Changing the width of cells to accommodate the data

If a cell is too narrow for its numerical contents, a row of hash characters '####' will appear. You can widen the whole column by positioning the cursor over the dividers to the column headers so that the cursor becomes a double-headed arrow (as in Figure C16). You can then drag the border to an appropriate width by holding down the left-hand mouse button as you reposition the arrow. Columns can also be narrowed by the same method.

**Figure C16 The double-headed arrow**

### C4.2.2 Merging cells to create headings

If you want to create a heading for your worksheet you can select the required cells and click the 'Merge & Center' icon in the 'Home' ribbon shown in Figure C17

('*Home/Merge and Center*'). You can also do this via '**Ctrl+1**' and then selecting '*Merge cells*' (see Figure C17) before centring the text across the merged cells.

## C4.3 Formatting text and aligning data

You can only change the font in cells that have been selected. Many of the formatting options are similar to those in *Word* (such as bold, italic, underline, font size and style), and are

**Figure C17 The Merge Cells icon**

available from the small formatting menu that appears after right-clicking over the cell or, alternatively, via the icons in the 'Font' and 'Alignment' groups in the 'Home' ribbon. However, a wider range of options is available for formatting the border, patterns, alignment and text orientation within the cells, through the 'Format Cells' dialogue box, as shown in Figure C18. This dialogue box can be activated quickly by right-clicking on the selected cells and choosing '*Format Cells*' from the shortcut menu. The box can also be reached by other routes, such as by using the little arrows at the bottom of the 'Font' and 'Alignment' groups of the 'Home' ribbon or by

selecting '*Format Cells*' at the bottom of the '*Format*' sub-menu (found in the 'Cells' group).

In *Excel*, numbers are conventionally aligned to the right of the cell and text at the left; however, you can alter this either by using the alignment buttons in the 'Home' ribbon or via the '*Vertical*' and '*Horizontal*' options in the 'Format Cells' dialogue box. Additional options include the ability to assign numerical values monetary units and expressing values as percentages ('*Number*').

**Figure C18 The Format Cells dialogue box**

## C4.4 Borders and shading for impact

Presentation of data in spreadsheets can sometimes be improved by adding borders around specific cells or shading sections, as these can help to highlight titles, table headings, specific values, etc. To insert borders around a selected cell or an array of cells, click on the down-arrow next to the 'Borders' icon in the 'Home' ribbon and choose from the selection of border types

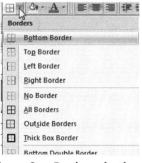

**Figure C19 Border selection**

that appear in the sub-menu, pictured in Figure C19. Areas of the spreadsheet can also be highlighted by filling them with colour, and the 'Fill Color' icon in the 'Home' ribbon provides various options for this, as shown in Figure C20. Note that these options can also be reached via the 'Format Cells' dialogue box. More fancy presentation options are available via the 'Styles' group, but do remember that to present data clearly usually does not require a variety of gimmicky effects.

**Figure C20  Colour selection**

# C5  Producing charts and graphs

You can easily convert data in *Excel* spreadsheets into graphs by selecting from the options in the 'Charts' group of the 'Insert' ribbon. It is important to choose the most appropriate way of illustrating your data and, for scientific representations, the most useful charts are likely to be line, bar or column graphs and also scatter charts. Pie charts can also be useful and sometimes 3D charts can give more of an impact. Make sure you give the rows and columns appropriate names and include these names when you select the data, so that the chart can be appropriately labelled.

## C5.1  Creating a simple scatter chart

A scatter chart with a best-fit line is appropriate for several sets of data measured against one variable, such as the growth rate of different groups against time, the degree of response over a range of conditions, the rates of an enzyme reaction under different conditions, and the extent of binding with pH. To start, select the data to be presented; in Figure C21 the data are in the columns headed 'pH' and 'Binding of Compound 1' (make sure you include the headings of the columns). Then, choose 'Scatter' from the 'Charts' group in the 'Insert' ribbon, as illustrated in Figure C22. Once you have made your choice, an

| | A | B |
|---|---|---|
| | *pH* | *Binding of Compound 1 (mmol)* |
| 1 | | |
| 2 | *5* | *0.07* |
| 3 | *6* | *0.159* |
| 4 | *7* | *0.099* |
| 5 | *8* | *0.045* |
| 6 | *9* | *0.01* |

**Figure C21  Selection of data**

illustration of the chart will appear (such as the one shown in Figure C23, derived from the data in Figure C21) and at the same time the three 'Chart Tools' tabs: 'Design', 'Layout' and 'Format', become visible. The 'Design' ribbon provides a choice of standard layouts (in the 'Chart Layout' group) and styles for the data points (in the 'Chart Styles' group). Although the 'Format' ribbon provides a variety of quite fancy options for presenting your data, do remember that over-use

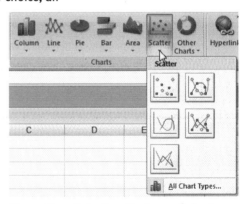

**Figure C22  Selecting the type of chart**

of the more decorative formatting options can be a distraction and could reduce the impact of your chart.

**Binding of Compound 1 (mmol)**

**Figure C23  The initial plot**

You may want to make adjustments to improve the presentation, such as specifying a different range of data or altering the range of the axes so that the plot fits more neatly onto the chart area. There are various routes for making adjustments to your chart, the quickest usually being to right-click over the part you wish to change and then selecting the appropriate facility from the shortcut menu. In the sections below, some of the longer routes are also included to help you understand the options offered in the ribbons.

## C5.1.1  Adjusting the data

To adjust the range of cells included in your chart manually, you must use the 'Select Data Source' dialogue box (illustrated in Figure C24), which is activated either by right-clicking over one of the axes and selecting 'Select Data', or via 'Select Data' in the 'Design' ribbon. The addresses of the cells used to produce the graph and the number of the worksheet

**Figure C24  Selecting the source data**

that contains the data appear in the 'Chart data range' window. You can see in Figure C24 that the data range is represented as: '=Sheet5! $A$1:$B$6'[12], which means that the data are in worksheet 5 (Sheet5!) and the data range starts at A1 ($A$1) and ends at B6 ($B$6). The 'Switch Row/Column' button indicates how Excel has grouped the data. In this example the data are arranged in columns so that the 'Horizontal (Category) Axis Labels' contains the first column of data

---

12  A note about the dollar signs. Typically, cell references are 'relative' so that if the formula in a cell is copied or cut and pasted to another location, the cell references will move to cells that are placed in the same relative position to those in the original location. You can, however, make reference to absolute positions. By placing a dollar sign before the letter in the cell reference, no matter where the formula may be copied, the column position will be absolute, thus '$A' will always refer to cells in Column A. Likewise, placing a dollar sign before the number in a cell reference will fix reference to that particular row, so that $4 will refer to a cell in row 4. Placing a dollar sign before both the letter and the number in a cell reference will fix both the column and the row position, thus $A$4 will always refer to the cell in row 4 of the first column of a spreadsheet, no matter where its formula gets copied.

(the independent variable set) that should appear along the *x*-axis. If, however, your data are organized in rows, then you would need to click on '*Switch Row/ Column*' so that the data you want to place along the horizontal axis appear under 'Horizontal (Category) Axis Labels' instead of under 'Legend Entries (Series)'.

## C5.1.2 Adjusting the axes

If, as in our example in Figure C23, the data are squashed to one side of the graph, you might want to change the range of the axis (the *x*-axis in this case) to give a more balanced look. You can reset the maximum and minimum values by right-clicking over one of the numbers in that axis and choosing '*Format Axis*' from the shortcut menu. This allows you to see the 'Format Axis' dialogue box shown in Figure C25. An alternative way to reach this box is via 'Axis' in the 'Layout' ribbon and then selecting '*Primary Vertical (Horizontal) Axis / More Primary Vertical (Horizontal) Axis Options*'. In Figure C25 the pH range along the *x*-axis has been adjusted to start at 4, by deselecting 'Auto' for the Minimum Axis Options and inserting the value 4. The effect of this on the plot in Figure C23 is shown in Figure C26.

**Figure C25 The Format Axis dialogue box**

The 'Format Axis' dialogue box also allows you to set the units along the axes at appropriate intervals.

**Figure C26 The repositioned plot**

Note that this dialogue box contains other options including creating a logarithmic scale along one or both axes and also provides options for altering the style of the line and fonts ('*Number*', '*Fill*', '*Line Color*', '*Line Style*', etc).

## C5.1.3 Adding titles, legends and labels

The 'Labels' group in the 'Layout' ribbon allows you to include approriate titles, legends, labels for axes and individual data points. Clicking on any of these options provides you with a sub-menu that lets you select an appropriate position on the chart. Figure C27 shows the sub-menu for 'Chart Title'. The text in the title and axes labels can be changed by clicking over the text to select it

**Figure C27 Inserting a Chart Title**

(small dots will appear at the corners of the text box to show it has been activated) and then simply editing the contents of the box. An alternative way to re-word the title or legends is by right-clicking over the relevant portion and selecting '*Edit Text*' from the shortcut menu as shown in Figure C28.

**Figure C28 Editing an axis label**

If the standard positions given by *Excel* need adjusting, you can reposition individual chart components by simply selecting them and then dragging and dropping them into a new position.

## C5.1.4 *Saving your chart*

Once you are satisfied with your basic chart you can save it as an object in your existing worksheet or in a new worksheet via the '*Move Chart Location*' facility in the 'Design' ribbon. You are invited to give a name to the new worksheet so you can identify it easily in the future.

## C5.2 *More complicated scatter charts*

Where several different sets of data are being analysed, each of the different sets is contained within its individual series on the chart and represented as a separate line, as illustrated in Figure C29. Providing you included the names of the data sets (for example, the column headings) when selecting the data, you will see these names appear

**Figure C29 A scatter plot containing several data series**

in the legend (or key). *Excel* has default choices for line colours; these may be indistinguishable on a black and white printed page but you can modify the colour and style of the lines and data points by right-clicking over them (dark coloured circles will surround the selected data) then selecting '*Format data series*', as shown in Figure C30, which takes you to the 'Format Data Series' dialogue box.

**Figure C30 Formatting the data series**

## C5.3 *Switching to a different type of chart*

If you decide that your data would be represented better in a different format, you can do this by right-clicking over the chart area and selecting '*Change Chart Type*' in the shortcut menu. (An alternative route to this facility is via '*Change Chart Type*' in the 'Design' ribbon.) By exploring the various possibilities you will discover the most appropriate format for representing the data. For example, the data in Figure C29 can be represented as a

Effect of pH on binding of Compounds 1,2 and 3

**Figure C31  A histogram**

histogram pictured in Figure C31. The colours and patterns of the chart can again be changed using the formatting options available in the shortcut menus that appear after right-clicking over each element of the chart.

---

**Note**

If you alter the data in the *Excel* spreadsheet from which the chart has been created, the chart will also change to take into account the modified data.

---

## C5.4  Inserting trendlines

If you have initially chosen a scatter chart *without* a smooth line drawn by *Excel*, and want to insert a trendline, *Excel* will calculate its position for you. To do this, left-click over one of the data points so that the points become surrounded by dark circles, then right-click to see the shortcut menu shown in Figure C30. Choose '*Add Trendline*'. If your points do not have a linear relationship, *Excel* will offer you various options (shown in Figure C32); if no obvious mathematical relationship is apparent, choose '*Moving Average*'. If you want to remove a trendline, select it (by clicking over it once), and press the '**Delete**' key.

*Excel* will also calculate a linear regression formula and an *R*-squared value on suitable plots

**Figure C32  The Format Trendline dialogue box**

if you select '*Display Equation on chart*' and/or '*Display R-squared value on chart*', as illustrated in Figure C32. Another route to this function is via 'Trendline' in the 'Analysis' group of the 'Layout' ribbon.

---

**Warning:** ALWAYS check that the trendline offered by *Excel* is sensible; if you have anomalous data the trendline offered may not give a true representation of the actual trend!

---

## C5.5 Inserting error bars

Error bars can easily be inserted into your chart using the 'Format Error Bars' dialogue box, illustrated in Figure C33. This is obtained by choosing '*Error Bars*' in the 'Analysis' group of the 'Layout' ribbon. There are several standard options which allow you to set the length of all the error bars to represent such things as standard errors, standard deviations, range, etc. but if you select '*Custom*' then '*Specify Value*', the 'Custom Error Bars' box that appears (as shown in Figure C33) allows you to set individual values for each of the data points in turn. If you need to adjust the bars you can do so by first clicking over the data point to select it, and then right-clicking over the existing error bar to activate it. The shortcut menu that appears provides a '*Format Error Bar*' option.

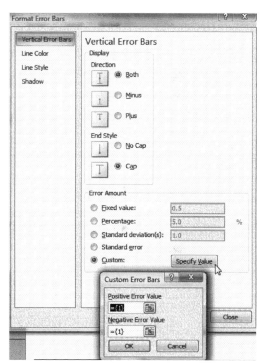

**Figure C33  Inserting error bars**

---

**Note**

If you want to specify different length error bars for each data point but find that all the columns or bars simultaneously gain the same length as you enter the values, you should right-click over the chart and choose '*Select Data*' from the sub-menu that appears. Then click on the '*Switch Row/Column*' button. This ensures that each column or bar represents a different data series (and is shown in a different colour or pattern) each with its own range and errors.

## C5.6  *Other types of chart*

Representing some types of data as pie charts can be effective (for example, in the composition of fluids or populations of species in different habitats) and 3D effects for line charts and histograms can sometimes be used for impact. If you choose a 3D format, do make sure that valuable data do not get hidden. If you decide that your data would be more clearly represented in a different type of chart you should right-click over your chart to see the shortcut menu, then select '*Change Chart Type*' to see the different options available.

# Index